# Terry W Browne

# Playwrights' Theatre

## The English Stage Company at the Royal Court Theatre

With Foreword by Martin Esslin

D1447594

Pitman Pu

First published 1975

PITMAN PUBLISHING LTD
Pitman House, 39 Parker Street, London WC2B 5PB, UK

PITMAN MEDICAL PUBLISHING CO LTD
42 Camden Road, Tunbridge Wells, Kent TN1 2QD, UK

FOCAL PRESS LTD
31 Fitzroy Square, London W1P 6BH, UK

PITMAN PUBLISHING CORPORATION
6 East 43 Street, New York, NY 10017, USA

FEARON PUBLISHERS INC
6 Davis Drive, Belmont, California 94002, USA

PITMAN PUBLISHING PTY LTD
Pitman House, 158 Bouverie Street, Carlton, Victoria 3053, Australia

PITMAN PUBLISHING
COPP CLARK PUBLISHING
517 Wellington Street West, Toronto M5V 1G1, Canada

SIR ISAAC PITMAN AND SONS LTD
Banda Street, PO Box 46038, Nairobi, Kenya

PITMAN PUBLISHING CO SA (PTY) LTD
Craighall Mews, Jan Smuts Avenue, Craighall Park, Johannesburg 2001, South Africa

*Cased Edition* ISBN 0 273 00757 2
*Paperback Edition* ISBN 0 273 00758 0

Text set in 11 pt. Photon Imprint, printed by photolithography, and bound in Great Britain at The Pitman Press, Bath

G. 3549/3550:13

# foreword

Books which deal with the history of a theatre usually fall into the category of the cosily nostalgic. Their readers want to recall their own youth through wallowing in a hot bath of perfumed memories. There is a need for such books; and some of them are splendidly readable. This study of the phenomenon of the creation of a writers' theatre at the Royal Court pursues a different aim and will serve a different purpose.

It is not often that theatrical history becomes a factor in the mainstream of historical and social development. The history of the Royal Court under George Devine and his successors, however, can claim to have had such a major impact. The breakthrough Devine achieved for the new generation of English playwrights had a measurable influence on the social climate of Britain in the late fifties, sixties and seventies.

Advocates of a purely commercial theatre tend to claim that it is more democratic than a subsidized operation: the audiences vote with their purses for what they want to see and reject what they don't want. The fallacy of this argument stems from the fact that there is not one audience but many. Only a very small percentage of the population ever goes to the theatre – it has been estimated not to exceed between two and five per cent, even in countries with many more theatres than Britain and the U.S.A. possess – and once a certain type of play has built up a certain type of audience, success in commercial terms becomes a highly incestuous affair. The theatres cater for the known tastes of their known audience (and in the pre-Royal Court West End this was a certain type of middle-class audience) and the audience in turn rejects anything that is not to its taste. To break into this closed circle of cause and effect is impossible without the time needed to build up a new audience, that is: to attract people who do not expect there is anything they would like in the theatre, to make them aware of the existence of something that is to their taste and to create in them a habit of going to see such theatre – not to speak of the tastes and critical standards which have to be nurtured in such a new audience.

The achievement of the Royal Court under Devine was to have done just that. Admittedly, circumstances were unusually propitious. A new educated class was emerging in Britain through the effects of the educational and social revolution after the Second World War. This new educated class was also a new middle class and therefore conditioned to fall into such habitually middle-class pursuits as theatre-going. What the success – or *succès de scandale* of Osborne's *Look Back in Anger* revealed was the fact, hitherto unsuspected by the commercial entrepreneurs of the theatre, that plays dealing with lower class characters speaking a non-standard English and flouting the conventions of the 'who's-for-tennis' school of playwriting could actually become profitable theatrical ventures.

The long-term effects of this realization were far-reaching. They opened a whole range of subjects for discussion: the power of the theatre to inspire changes of public opinion should not be underestimated. The theatre provides one of the relatively few common grounds for conversation in a society like the English where politics as well as personal affairs are a conversational taboo. Such permissible subjects of conversation are eagerly seized upon by the newspapers and thus filter down into wider and wider strata of society. There can be no doubt that Ibsen did a great deal to change the image of the social role of women in late Victorian and Edwardian society. Similarly, the Royal Court dramatists had their impact on the liberalization of attitudes towards a whole range of society's outsiders and indeed in making moral attitudes in society at large more 'permissive'.

It is no coincidence that the development which ended in the abolition of stage censorship in Britain was sparked off by the two cases in which plays at the Royal Court were under attack by the authorities. I shall never forget the afternoon performance of Bond's *Early Morning* in 1968 to which only people who had been personally invited were admitted, by a side door and without payment, so that the wholly private character of the occasion could be preserved. The fact that the theatre pressing for a liberalization of the long obsolete and fossilized views of what an audience in the theatre could be exposed to was, at the same time, in receipt of encouragement and subsidy from the authorities, only highlighted the paradox of the case: the inner tension between the remnants of the past and the needs of the present in our society. Having been banned by one branch of the authorities from public performance, Bond's *Saved* was sent on a foreign tour by another section of the governmental structure (the British Council) as an example of the advanced and flourishing state of British culture.

That the generation – or rather generations, for there is a second wave of writers coming out of the Royal Court at this moment – of British playwrights which were nurtured by the Royal Court have greatly enhanced British prestige abroad is beyond doubt. Any study of the elements through which a nation acquires its international image and international standing would have to place a country's literature and drama very high on the list among its scientific, industrial and sporting achievements. In a period of steady decline of British power British artistic achievement has played an important part in keeping the country's prestige high. And in this area British playwrights – and their achievements on the stage, in the cinema and in the mass media – have been of paramount importance. In the development of these playwrights the Royal Court played a decisive role.

Nothing highlights the continued – and, indeed, vastly increased – influence of the theatre on the culture and life style of a nation more than the interaction between the living stage and the mechanically reproduced mass media, the cinema and television. The revolution initiated by the Royal Court in the subject matter and language of the stage has already had a vast impact through television and the cinema: Tony Richardson's film of *Tom Jones* in which George Devine played Squire Allworthy, for which John Osborne wrote the script and in which a whole gallery of Royal Court actors featured, carried the Royal Court into all corners of the world and won world-wide acclaim. The best of British television drama, with its social relevance, frankness of language and boldness in the choice of subject matter, has made what seemed the breakthroughs of a numerically insignificant avant-garde of highbrows the daily pabulum of millions and millions of viewers throughout the United Kingdom. The impact of such a fact on the cultural climate of the nation must be immense, whether for good or for ill. Those who are convinced that artistic truth in drama has a humanizing influence will argue that a gradual improvement in the mass public's ability to confront, understand and enjoy realistic and sharp portrayals of actual, complex human situations, instead of feeble-minded and stereotyped fantasies, will ultimately result in a more adult and more humane society.

It is from considerations such as these that I should like to suggest that a phenomenon like Devine's creation at the Royal Court is more than merely a picturesque facet of theatrical history but a highly significant social and cultural development worthy of detailed and thorough investigation.

Terry Browne's book has assembled an impressive array of factual material, meticulously documented, from which important insights into the genesis of a theatrical movement and its multifarious connections with the development of the society and culture surrounding it, emerge with great clarity. It is not only valuable to have this record to give one an understanding of the past, it also contains many lessons for the future.

Martin Esslin

For Carol

# Preface

A study of the history of the English Stage Company at the Royal Court Theatre has obviously been needed. In its eighteen years of existence the Company has produced over 250 plays, the majority of them new plays by British authors. Although the Royal Court is a writers' theatre, it would be ludicrous to attempt to dissect or even to comment upon each production, or even to attempt to trace the artistic or thematic development of the more prominent playwrights. While the latter approach to the subject is fascinating, it is also limiting. The thrust of my approach has been to trace the history of the theatre which made that development and those productions possible.

A theatre is a reflection of the people who run it. The longer that group stays together, the stronger and more clear becomes that reflection. And that reflection will be more and more of the strongest personality involved. It is beyond the scope of this study to deal at length with the diverse, sometimes warring, personalities involved with the history of the English Stage Company; but their reflection, the theatre itself, will tell of them, will show what stuff they were and are made of. Though their aims were sometimes distorted by circumstances, economic and social, that only serves to show more facets of those remarkable and very human people. The lives and loves of the personalities involved in the Royal Court are not the concern of this book; their common love, the image of their personalities – the English Stage Company itself – is the concern.

Because little factual material has been published about the English Stage Company, there was no way to find the answers to the questions involved except to study first-hand the day-to-day workings of the theatre; to delve into the Company's records; and to talk with both those involved in its founding and development and those who are presently actively involved in the Company. I am therefore happy to express my thanks to the late Neville Blond, C.M.G., O.B.E., Lindsay Anderson, Dennis Andrews, J. Edward Blacksell, M.B.E., John Blatchley, Howard Brenton, Pamela Brighton, Lena Cope, Roger Croucher, Ronald Duncan, Antonia Davy, the late Robin Fox, M.C., William Gaskill, Jocelyn Herbert, Patricia Lawrence, Oscar Lewenstein, John Osborne, Anthony Page, Greville Poke, Glen Byam Shaw, Max Stafford-Clark, Tony Richardson, and Nicholas Wright for their help, and to Jon Catty for his help with the financial tables and for his very useful advice throughout. Special thanks to Richard Fallon and Dr. Arthur Dorlag for their support and suggestions. Finally, I thank my friend and mentor Martin Esslin, whose constant encouragement and guidance have been invaluable.

T.W.B.

# Contents

# 1 The founding

The need for such an organization as the English Stage Company at the Royal Court Theatre, now in its fame popularly referred to as the Royal Court or simply as the Court, was felt by all serious-minded theatre people in London. However, the actual organization began in the south-western rural county of Devon.

In the early 1950s Ronald Duncan, the Earl of Harewood, James Edward Blacksell and Benjamin Britten had founded the Devon Festival, then known as the Taw and Torridge Festival. In its first year, 1953, the festival was well attended, but not financially successful. There were no major problems with the music side of the festival; the drama part of the programme, however, provided more difficulties. One of them was finding actors and producers interested in presenting plays at a festival. There weren't any companies of any quality, and individual actors didn't like working so far away from London, especially not for such a short time as one or two weeks. Managements, quite rightly in Duncan's opinion, pointed out that to play for a week or a fortnight at a festival was uncommercial: they could not recoup production costs and festival guarantees were insufficient to cover their inevitable deficit. The plays which the festival wanted to produce would have little chance of transferring into London.

The following year the same problems persisted. There was a dearth of new plays from which to choose: the playwrights obviously couldn't make much money under such circumstances, and it was obvious that quality of production was unattainable under such handicaps. It was then that the idea of forming a management which would devote itself to producing non-commercial plays began to develop strength.

The group of men who came together with the common purpose of founding this new management certainly seemed disparate. Lord Harewood, son of the Princess Royal and cousin of the Queen, had long had an active interest in the arts and was a trained musicologist with an M.A. from Cambridge. He had helped to found the English Opera Group and had served on the councils of many artistic enterprises, especially those concerned with music. His name was important, since it would serve to attract contributions and would give the organization a definite aura of respectability. But, besides allowing his name to be used, Lord Harewood also had a very real interest in the improvement of the arts, and has since served as President of the Royal Shakespeare Theatre, as a director of the Royal Opera House, Covent Garden, and as Artistic Director of the Edinburgh Festival from 1961 to 1965.

James Edward Blacksell, master of a large boys' school in Barnstaple, had begun his association with the others with the founding of the Devon Festival. He was an enthusiastic organizer and was later to offer an introduction which would provide one of the people most important to the success of the English Stage Company.

Although Ronald Duncan has written or adapted eighteen plays and is the author of eleven prose books, he is best known for his work in the poetic theatre movement centred around the Mercury Theatre in the early 1950s. His verse play *This Way to the Tomb* ran in the West End of London for eighteen months. Another great success, which also ran in the West End for over a year, was his free adaptation of Cocteau's *Azarel* (*The Angel of Death*) which Duncan retitled *The Eagle Has Two Heads*. He is also known for his work as librettist with Benjamin Britten (principally, perhaps, for *The Rape of Lucretia*). Oscar Lewenstein, without guile, described him as he was then as 'high church, right-wing, anarchist'. Perhaps 'idealist' would be a better term than 'anarchist', with all its present-day wild-eyed connotations. At any rate, he had had a very interesting career: he had lived and worked with Ghandi for a year in India; he had been a pacifist; he had worked in the coal mines of England and had led workers on a march to London to protest about their conditions; he had had three plays running in the West End simultaneously; he had been instrumental in founding the English Opera Group and, as already mentioned, the Devon Festival. About 1953, Duncan had had the idea to hire a theatre and put on a season of new plays, his own and those of others. When seeking a theatre he met Oscar Lewenstein, then working as manager of the Royal Court Theatre. Although nothing came of that scheme, the meeting was propitious.

Oscar Lewenstein, a man with ferocious energy, came from a branch of the theatre completely different from the poetic movement of the Mercury Theatre. He came up through the Glasgow Unity Theatre, a left-wing, socially committed group, which, during the 1930s, did such things as Odets and O'Casey plays and was very much in favour of the agit-prop utilitarian philosphy of theatre. Immediately after the Second World War there were about twenty of these amateur groups in Great Britain and Lewenstein became the national organizer. The London and Glasgow groups were quite strong and about 1946 they turned professional. Lewenstein then went to Glasgow as a general manager, where they produced Miller, O'Casey, and Gorky. The Glasgow Unity Theatre took a season of plays to London and Lewenstein remained to enter the commercial theatre as manager of the Embassy Theatre, Swiss Cottage, London. He then moved on to become the general manager of the Royal Court, which Alfred Esdaile had leased. It was while in that position that he began to talk with Duncan and the idea to form a management for the presentation of the works of serious contemporary writers began to become a solid reality.

There is dispute over just who first suggested the actual founding of the English Stage Company. Blacksell says that the resolve was born in a conversation among the principals which took place in his house. Duncan says that he had had the idea as early as 1947 and that he, in 1954, with the help of his wife, Rose Marie, and his secretary,

Antonia Davy, began the process of raising interest and support, and that Blacksell quickly supported the venture and began drafting an appeal to the Arts Council. Lewenstein says that the idea, which had been brewing in him for some time, came into the open in a conversation with Duncan: Lewenstein was visiting Duncan at his Devon farm and in a conversation while walking on the beach they decided to form a theatre where serious contemporary plays could be done. No doubt all these views of the beginnings are true. The determination to undertake such a project does not spring to life in one conversation. Duncan had said the year before that the furthering of new and different plays could be undertaken by Civic Theatres which 'are as necessary as public lavatories.' Oscar Lewenstein had already formed a commercial producing company with Wolf Mankowitz to raise money in the orthodox way to put on serious plays. Blacksell was aware of the difficulties not only of putting on plays at the festival, but of even finding worthwhile new works to put on. Lord Harewood was aware of the need for stimulation and, as always, was eager to help in providing that stimulation. It little matters who first suggested that they actually form the management; all were in agreement about the need and resolved to do something about fulfilling it.

Why was such a management needed, besides the desire to provide companies for the festivals? What was going on in the West End of London that was so unsatisfactory?

The commercial theatre of 1954–5 has been described as: 'a vast desert'; 'only interested in innocuous little plays which would provide a vehicle for a star to achieve a long and tedious run'; 'the end of an era'; 'fairly frivolous'. The list could go on and on. The impression remains that the commercial managements were fulfilling their task of providing entertainment which had a proven saleability. The task of the commercial manager is to make money for his backers. He is first a businessman and only secondly an artist. Faced with high production costs, it is natural that he should use his acumen to try to pick a play that will please the public so that the public will pay to see it. If, on that basis, he does not choose correctly often enough, he will not be a commercial manager for very long. Thus, he has two main guides in deciding on a play to produce. Firstly, he can choose something which is sufficiently like past successes to indicate that it is acceptable to the public – thus, the most decisive success of 1954–5 on every level was Enid Bagnold's glittering and artificial high comedy, *The Chalk Garden*, a play which could have been written at any time since Oscar Wilde. Secondly, the commercial manager can produce in London something which has already proved itself elsewhere, thus giving it a better – though not certain – chance of success. During the 1954–5 season, there were six imports from Paris and in May 1955 there were fourteen American shows of one kind or another playing in the West End. When questioned about this imbalance, the managers usually replied that the English plays simply were not there.[1]

The English were represented, of course. Ludovic Kennedy's *Murder Story* and Agatha Christie's *The Spider's Web* and *The Mousetrap* (which is still running) provided mysteries; there were a great number of sentimental English musicals, of which *Salad Days* was the outstanding success; and the Bard was at the Old Vic. Terence Rattigan again proved he was master of the West End with his *Separate Tables*. And there were a great number of forgotten light comedies and thrillers. The London theatre remained a middle-class theatre. The fare was dictated by the public and the public liked what was given to them. Coach tours deposited large numbers in from the suburbs and the provinces for an evening of pleasure in the West End and that pleasure was going to be safe: something they *knew* they would like; something proven in a long-run or abroad; something which had a star player in it. As T. C. Worsley pointed out:

> 'However genuinely anxious the commercial managements are to find new plays, the conditions under which they work operate against the original writer. If they do find an orginal play on which they are prepared to take a risk, they can only afford to do so when they have secured one or the other of the crowd-drawing stars to give them a second line of defence. The protracted delays and frequent frustrations which this involves often ends in sickening writers with the whole business, and they return to the comparatively sensibly organized world of publishing.'[2]

So the playwrights had to provide plays which not only fitted the accepted formula, but also provided star roles. The high salaries commanded by the stars added enormously to the already-high costs of production and placed further demands on the managements to have long runs. The theatres were flooded with business, but the long-run plays tied up theatres and made it even more difficult for a new play to get a hearing. There was certainly no place in the commercial system for plays of questionable commercial value, regardless of their artistic merits.

The problem of providing an outlet for new playwrights in the face of commercial conservatism was not a new one. In 1899 the Stage Society Incorporated was founded for the production of plays with artistic merit, but with little chance of presentation by a commercial management. The plays were to be given in a West End theatre with a West End cast for one or two performances, usually on Sundays. The Society's productions, which numbered over 200 during its lifetime, included the first production in England of a number of Shaw's plays, as well as plays by such foreign dramatists at Hauptmann, Gorky, Gogol, Wedekind, Kaiser, Pirandello, J. J. Bernard, Cocteau, and Odets. The Stage Society continued its activities until the outbreak of the Second World War, after which it was not revived. The 1904–7 Vedrenne-Barker seasons at the Royal Court Theatre, which will be dealt with in more detail later, grew out of the Stage Society's activities.

In 1945, Henry Sherek, with the encouragement of the newly-formed Arts Council of Great Britain, formed the non-profit-distributing company Sherek Plays, Ltd, with the policy of 'the presentation of new English plays, with a bias towards those of special contemporary interest'. The ultimate aim was a programme of three or four plays performed in repertoire by a permanent company. However, when tried, the actors would not submit to the unfamiliar repertory system and that plan had to be scrapped. Of the fourteen plays produced by Sherek during six years' association with the Arts Council, ten were new plays by British authors. The major contribution to British theatre was the production of T. S. Eliot's *The Cocktail Party* at the Edinburgh Festival in 1949 and later in the West End; but with Eliot as the author and Alec Guinness playing the lead, this hardly showed daring.

On 5 October 1945, The Company of Four – Tennent's, Glyndebourne Opera Company, the Cambridge Arts Theatre, and Tyrone Guthrie – opened their occupation of the Lyric Theatre, Hammersmith. Its objectives were to give opportunities to new playwrights, young actors, and directors. Glyndebourne and Guthrie withdrew their support after the first year and the Cambridge Arts Theatre withdrew in 1950, leaving Tennents with full responsibility. During its six years of association with the Arts Council, which ended in 1951, the Lyric had forty-seven productions of which only eighteen were plays by British or Irish authors not previously produced in Great Britain; and, of the fifteen plays which were transferred into the West End during that period, only two were new plays by unknown authors. While the Lyric was an important vitalizing element in English theatre, it could not accurately be called experimental. It served mainly as a tryout theatre for H. M. Tennent Productions, Ltd. Its plays were put on always with an eye to transfer into the West End. That caused a certain amount of conservatism in their choice of plays and players.

The Old Vic introduced an even more ambitious scheme for the improvement of theatre in 1946 when they announced the Old Vic Theatre Centre. The Centre was to have a school for intensive and experimental training in theatre; a company, the Young Vic, was to provide an outlet for the actors and provide an attraction for other theatrical artists; and, finally, a flexible centre was to be constructed in which to house the project. At first they would draw from existing plays, but their intention was to attract dramatists and other artists and eventually to build up a repertory of new plays and adaptations. The whole scheme was to aim at giving a solid working background to the new and experimental in the theatre.

The scheme had Michel Saint-Denis as administrator in charge, Glen Byam Shaw as director of the school, and George Devine as director of the Young Vic. All three of these great men of the theatre, apart from their proven artistic abilities, had a great sense of public duty and idealism. It is important to note the philosophy which directed them in their work:

'We were "ensembliers". We set out to develop initiative, freedom, and a sense of responsibility in the individual, as long as he or she was ready and able to merge his personal qualities into the ensemble.

'We never worked from or towards a system . . .

'The school was always partly experimental, but to avoid conceit and extravagance we maintained that our chief practical purpose was wholly and above all to serve interpretation, and that in

dealing with an important play it was healthy to consider the
author as the only completely creative person: director, designer,
and actor had to understand the author's intention and submit to
it.'[3]

Although the School and the Young Vic certainly achieved some
success, they were never able to fulfil themselves. The money was not
found to build the Centre and, finally, there was not enough to
finance the School and the Young Vic. The governors of the Old Vic
decided in the spring of 1951 to disband the Young Vic forthwith and
the Theatre School in the summer of 1952. Of the Centre, there was
nothing but the reconstructed stage.

At the same time, in the early 1950s, the theatre clubs and small
try-out theatres were closing one by one: the Watergate, the New
Lindsey, the Boltons, the Q. Only the Arts Theatre remained with
sufficient facilities to do justice to a difficult new work. But the Arts,
though a vital force, was a small club theatre with consequently
limited audience.

So, in spite of some worthwhile attempts to provide centres of
revitalization for the theatre, by 1955 there were no major theatre
companies willing to take on experimental work. *Plays and Players*
commented:

'Despairingly theatre-lovers have been asking for years where our
new dramatists are to be found.
   '. . . The blame for this sad state of affairs has been variously
distributed. Managements say that the serious plays submitted to
them by British dramatists are not worthy of being staged; indignant authors complain that managements refuse to consider their
excursions into the field of significant drama, while certain
progressive opinion holds that the routine realism of our existing
theatrical conventions does not exert any great appeal for writers
of imagination. But whatever the cause, there has certainly been
little encouragement of new talent.'[4]

The English Stage Company, by 1955 in the initial stages of formation, was preparing to step boldly into this tremendous gap in
English theatre. At that time the founders wanted to have a management to produce the great modern writers, such as Miller and Brecht
(Brecht was practically unknown on the English stage). They didn't
know that there were any particularly great modern writers in
England, but it was hoped that if a hospitable production company
could be formed the writers would appear. With this hope and the
hopes of providing a company to tour festivals, the organization
began to gel.

The first step was to form the Council. Besides Duncan, Blacksell,
Lewenstein and Lord Harewood, it was decided to ask Alfred
Esdaile, lessee of the Royal Court Theatre, to join. Lewenstein
thought he would be intrigued with the idea of the English Stage
Company, and Lewenstein also wanted to use the Royal Court as a
headquarters for the Council – although there was no intention of
acquiring that theatre – or any theatre – at that time. But it would
make the Council feel more real to be based in a theatre. Sir Reginald

Kennedy-Cox, Chairman of the Salisbury Arts Theatre and a friend of Duncan, joined the Council and donated £2,000, with the proviso that the money be used to produce Duncan's *Don Juan* and *The Death of Satan* in the first year. Eric Duncannon, now Lord Bessborough, and Greville Poke, former publisher of *Everybody's* magazine, were also asked to join the Council. Both were keenly interested in theatre and neither, according to Duncan, 'had any axe to grind of their own'. They were the sort of stable, respected men in whom the Arts Council tends to place confidence. Greville Poke also had been involved with an earlier experimental repertory theatre which put on plays in a barn in Shere in the 1930s. The rule of that organization had been that they would not produce any play that had been performed in England before. Although during its first years it was the kind of theatre which would perform as long as the audience consisted of at least two members, it did achieve some fame in the late 1930s as the summer theatre of Michel Saint-Denis's London Theatre Studio. So Greville Poke not only 'had no axe to grind', but was vitally interested in, and brought valuable experience to, the new project.

It was decided to call the new organization The English Stage Society, to correspond roughly with the English Opera Group which had been formed with essentially the same objectives for opera as the new group had for drama. However, Sir Vincent Truebridge, a reader of long standing in the Lord Chamberlain's Office, pointed out the parallel with the earlier Stage Society and though it was in poor taste to trade on that name and reputation. The Council had never intended to do so and readily changed the name of their organization to The English Stage Company.

In the autumn of 1955 the decision to form a management had been taken, an impressive Council had been formed, and the Company had been incorporated and had become, in legal reality, The English Stage Company. But existence as a legal reality and existence as a working reality are often not the same thing. What were the assets and aims of the fledgling English Stage Company at this point?

The aims were to stage plays for festivals, produce uncommercial works, and commission the writing of plays. The intention was to rent a small theatre, such as the Embassy or the Westminster, and try to raise enough money to do one season of plays.

The resources were somewhat slim. The Arts Council had promised a grant of £500, Sir Reginald Kennedy-Cox had promised £2,000 for production of the Duncan plays, Greville Poke had provided an unsecured loan of £500 (and a few months later loaned an additional £2,326 for the purchase of lighting equipment), and about £500 had been raised from various other sources. So, the financial resources totalled about £3,500 with £2,000 already earmarked for production. The Council was certainly enthusiastic and substantial, but the only men with experience in professional theatre were Duncan and Lewenstein.

They did have plays to produce. Duncan and Blacksell had acquired the rights to Brecht's *The Threepenny Opera* for £100, and wanted to stage that, followed by *Waiting for Godot*.

Lewenstein had shown Duncan *Waiting for Godot* at the beginning of the summer and Duncan had recognized its worth immediately. Lewenstein said that every commercial management had rejected the play and the rights could be bought for £100. Duncan tried to arouse interest in the play, but was unable to find anyone who would provide the backing necessary for production. Eventually the Arts Theatre took it up and it became a surprise success of the 1955–6 season.

The history of *The Threepenny Opera* is more complex and, in its way, had a more profound influence – certainly on the English Stage Company. Again Duncan tried to arouse interest and raise money. He wrote to Olivier and didn't receive a reply. He talked with Gielgud who thought the play was 'a trifle sordid and a tedious bore'. The original plan to stage *The Threepenny Opera* at the 1955 Devon Festival had to be dropped. In its place, Joan Littlewood accepted the invitation to produce and play the title role in *Mother Courage*. Although the production was not a success, it was of tremendous import and certainly demonstrated the artistic tastes and courage of the founders of the English Stage Company. Brecht, though known in England in texts, had not been produced in Britain since before the war. *The Threepenny Opera* was taken up by Oscar Lewenstein who eventually was able to produce it at the Royal Court Theatre, by arrangement with the English Stage Company, as a pre-opening production, opening on 9 February 1956. It was another 'surprise' success and transferred to the Aldwych Theatre on 31 March, just two days before the opening of the English Stage Company's first production. For its role of associate producer the English Stage Company received one per cent of the weekly gross and, after transfer, one-half-of-one per cent. Thus, even before the opening of the English Stage Company's first season, the men involved had begun their programme of encouraging the best in theatre and had begun to shake the complacent assumptions of the West End managements.

In the spring of 1955 a step was taken which was to have a profound effect on the shape and future of the English Stage Company. Lord Harewood had been offered the Chairmanship of the Company, but declined and said that he thought it better that a rich businessman be brought in, although he didn't have anyone to suggest. Edward Blacksell, however, did.

During the Second World War Blacksell had been in the Royal Air Force and, with the plastic surgeon Sir Archibald McIndoe, had helped to found the Guinea Pig Club, which patched up airmen who had been badly burned during military operations. One of the major supporters of the Club was Neville Blond, a Manchester businessman. Blond, a rich man in his own right, was married to Elaine Marks, heiress of the Marks and Spencer chain store millions. Together, they had raised funds to found the Victoria Hospital.

Neville Blond, a man with extraordinary executive ability, had had a remarkable career. As a major in the Royal Horse Guards in World War I, he had been awarded the *Croix de Guerre avec Palme* and was made an *Officier de la Légion d'Honneur*. After the war he remained as Liaison Officer, *Ministere de la Guerre*, Paris, from 1918 to 1921. He then returned to the family business, Blond Brothers Textiles

Manufacturers, in Manchester. With the outbreak of the Second World War, he became Wing Commander in the Royal Air Force Fighter Command, and then joined the Ministry of Production from 1942 to 1945 and spent much of his time in Washington negotiating lend-lease, for which services he received the C.M.G. in 1945. After the war he was on the Board of Trade and then, in 1947, on the Central Economic Planning Staff. After that he served as the United Kingdom Trade Advisor to the United States from 1948 through 1949; then as Honourable Trade Advisor to the Board of Trade on North American Exports, from which he resigned in 1951 to become the Special Trade Advisor to the High Commissioner in Canada. In 1951 he received the O.B.E. in recognition of his services. However, he had had no connection with theatre and didn't claim any knowledge of theatre. Blond was still very active with his own company, but when approached by Blacksell he expressed interest in the English Stage Company and accepted an invitation to attend a meeting of the Council. He was impressed by the thoroughness of the organization and by the fact that the Company was using the same solicitors as he did. He then said he would attend another meeting if invited, and, after that second meeting, agreed to accept the Chairmanship, upon condition that a theatre be taken as a home for the company.

The Council was delighted with the idea of having its own theatre, but pointed out that it had very little money. However, Blond was now in his own element. He didn't claim to understand the artistic side of the theatre, but he did understand business and finance, and business and finance apply to theatre as much as to any business. As it happened, Alfred Esdaile, lessee of the Royal Court Theatre, also owned the Kingsway Theatre, which had been badly damaged by bombs during the Second World War and not repaired or reopened since. Esdaile agreed to lease the Kingsway to the English Stage Company, and Blond set about raising (and putting up) guarantees for the mortgage and for repairs.

With the promise of a permanent home for the Company and with the financial stability brought by Blond, it was obvious that the Company itself must have a permanence of organization. The first step was to find an artistic director.

Early in his tenancy of the Royal Court, Alfred Esdaile had been approached by George Devine and a young television director, Tony Richardson. They, too, thought that the British theatre was barren and they knew quite a lot of very good plays that never had a possibility of being produced commercially. They had the idea of forming a management which, in the words of Tony Richardson,

> 'would show a repertoire of modern plays and the possibilities of modern theatre, and which would also present plays which hadn't been produced in England, with the belief – and it was absolutely only a belief at that time – that this would produce a kind of renaissance of writing inside England'.

A wealthy woman had agreed to back them and they had worked out a whole scheme of the repertoire and all the things they wanted to do.

Unfortunately, the woman turned out to be merely a dilettante and the backing never in fact materialized, so the scheme had to be dropped.

Lewenstein had heard about this approach and suggested to the Council that Devine might be interested in becoming Artistic Director. Lewenstein didn't know Devine well – he had only met him once or twice – but he knew of him and thought he would be the ideal man for the job.

Devine, born in 1910, had had an interesting career in theatre. As a student at Oxford he became President of the O.U.D.S., the university dramatic organization. In that capacity he was instrumental in inviting Sir John Gielgud to Oxford in 1932 to produce and star in *Romeo and Juliet*, in which Peggy Ashcroft played Juliet and Edith Evans played the Nurse, with Devine playing Mercutio. Later the same year he made his professional debut in *The Merchant of Venice* at the St James Theatre, London. He then spent a season at the Old Vic and was then again associated with Gielgud in *Hamlet*. From 1936–9 Devine, besides various acting assignments, was a teacher and producer at the London Theatre Studio, founded by Michel Saint-Denis, with whom Devine had worked during his season at the Old Vic. The London Theatre Studio, founded in 1936, was based on the Copeau system of actor training, essentially the same philosophy upon which the Old Vic Theatre Centre was to be based. The Studio had given several productions and was a proven success by 1939, but the War forced it to close. After six years in the Army, Devine returned to the theatre and was again associated with Saint-Denis at the Old Vic School and as director of the Young Vic. The association had a profound influence on Devine. Always as idealist, he adopted the philosophy of Saint-Denis and was always interested in improving theatrical standards. This philosophy, of course, was to prove tremendously influential in the eventual shaping of the English Stage Company. Devine himself best summed up his attitude towards theatre when giving advice to his godson, who wanted to enter the British theatre:

'You should choose your theatre like you choose a religion. Make sure you don't get into the wrong temple. For me the theatre is really a religion or way of life. You must decide what you feel the world is about and what you want to say about it, so that everything in the theatre you work in is saying the same thing. This will be influenced partly by the man who is running it, and the actual physical and economic conditions under which he works . . .

'For me, the theatre is a temple of ideas and ideas so well expressed it may be called art. So always look for the quality in the writing above what is being said.

'This is how to choose a theatre to work in, and if you can't find one you like, start your own. A theatre must have a recognizable attitude. It will have one, whether you like it or not.'[5]

With his impressive background as recommendation and his earlier overtures to Esdaile as a suggestion of interest, it was agreed to approach Devine with the proposal. Lewenstein went to see Devine at the Westminster Theatre, where he was playing Tesman opposite Peggy Ashcroft in *Hedda Gabler*. Lewenstein talked with Devine in his dressing room between the matinée and evening performances, told him what was going on in the English Stage Company and asked him to join as Artistic Director. Devine was 'absolutely flabbergasted' that such a proposal should come to him from so unlikely a source. He didn't know any of the people connected with the enterprise and the only two people on the Council who were in the theatre were Duncan and Lewenstein. Lewenstein had no connection at that point with any of the more celebrated figures of the English theatre and had come up through a totally different kind of world from Devine's. As Lewenstein puts it, 'Somehow this was sort of a weird thing.' However, it was a serious proposition and Devine agreed to consider it. Duncan then had lunch with Devine and found that they were in complete agreement with the kind of drama which was needed to revitalize theatre. Devine agreed to meet the Council. At the Council meeting Devine said he would accept the position if Tony Richardson were invited to join as his associate. It was finally agreed, on 8 January 1956, to ask Richardson to become Assistant Artistic Director and that offer was accepted.

Only 27 years old in 1955, Richardson, another Oxford man, had been a television director at the B.B.C. since his graduation, and had directed the Free Cinema film *Momma Don't Allow*. He was to provide the 'flair' to complement Devine's experience.

After Devine and Richardson joined the Company it was decided that there should be an Artistic Committee and a Management Committee. The Artistic Committee, consisting of Duncan, Lewenstein, and Lord Harewood, as Chairman, was to choose the plays which were to be produced. They were to read all the plays and pass judgement on them, with the power of veto, before an option was taken by the Artistic Director. The Management Committee was to set budgets, decide on the programmes insofar as they needed consideration from a financial point of view, and would tend to the more mundane things, such as repairs, improvements, and the general operation of the theatre plant. The Council and its Chairman were, of course, to remain in final control. The Artistic Director who, though not a voting member, also attended the Council meetings was to make suggestions and generally guide the theatre, but always subject to the approval of the Council and Management and Artistic Committees. Although Neville Blond always maintained a tremendously strong control over the expenditure, in actual fact, George Devine had much more influence in the direction of the Court than an organizational chart would suggest. His experience and his own philosophy of theatre were bound to dominate. That domination was not always to come easily and led to some quite bitter disputes; but, although theatre is a group art, no effective producing organization can be run as a democracy by committee. It is a truism that 'a theatre must have a recognizable attitude, like it or not.' That attitude was to be forged by George Devine.

Plans for reconstructing the Kingsway Theatre were continued. Jocelyn Herbert designed and constructed a model of the stage. It was to be open, thrust, and flexible. £50,000 was allocated for the reconstruction of the theatre.

On 7 July 1955, at a reception in the shell of the Kingsway, the English Stage Company announced its existence and its intentions. There was still no roof over the stage and the auditorium was filled with rubble, but many notables of the theatre were there, including Gloria Swanson from America. George Devine made the announcement. He started and then stopped to clear his throat. In the pause Neville Blond thrust a glass into Devine's hand and boomed, 'Here, have a gin and tonic, George, and get on with it.'

The aims by this time had expanded beyond the original intentions. Besides touring the provincial theatres and festivals of the arts, it was now the intention of the English Stage Company to tour contemporary English plays abroad. This was in keeping with their basic intention of creating a new body of English writing for the theatre and creating an audience for that writing. They also planned to invite provincial repertory theatres to London to present new plays by English authors. Another aim was to attract novelists into the theatre. It was thought that novelists stayed away from theatre because of the difficulty involved in getting a play produced and that, if openly courted, they would respond with serious works for theatre. The Company were to go beyond simply enticing writers into the theatre with the promise of production: they wanted to find a contemporary style in dramatic work, acting, décor, and production. Thus, by presenting new or rarely seen foreign works in exciting productions, it was hoped to stimulate English authors. It was stressed in the original announcement and later reiterated to the press that 'we are not going in for experiment for the sake of experiment. We are not *avant-garde*, or highbrow, or a côterie set. We want to build a vital, living, *popular theatre*' [my italics]. The important fact that from the beginning the English Stage Company disavowed any intention of being *avant-garde* and stressed its aim of being a popular theatre is often forgotten in appraisals of its choice of plays and productions. Throughout its history, the Royal Court has been called not only 'left-wing' and 'radical', but also 'right-wing' and 'establishment' by those who would like to see it champion their own particular forms of experiment.

There was to be a permanent acting company and they would present plays in repertoire. It was hoped that this permanent company would afford the nucleus for experimenting in new methods of presentation and would carry out the aim of revitalizing the whole of English theatre; that it would, by working and experimenting as a group, develop a tradition, a style. By playing in repertoire it would also be possible to let successes carry those plays which proved less popular with audiences. This would be to the advantage of both the author and the Company: a play which might seem to be a popular failure under long-run conditions could possibly be nursed to success when in repertoire; likewise, those plays which proved popular successes could be fully exploited by the Company.

It must be remembered that the English Stage Company had very little money. When Neville Blond became Chairman, the pre-production grant from the Arts Council was raised to £2,500 and a subsidy of £7,000, including guarantees against loss, was granted for the first year of productions. Although Blond always guaranteed expenses, it was necessary for the Company to have a certain amount of financial success at the box office if it were to continue beyond the first year.

The press and critics reacted to the announcement with great enthusiasm. At first the joy was as much over the saving of the Kingsway at a time when so many theatres were being torn down as it was over the founding of a theatre for writers. But the purpose of the new Company was not lost. *The Times*, summing up the situation, said:

'While the Mercury, the Embassy, the "Q", the New Bolton, and the Watergate were still open he [the playwright] had a fighting chance of watching a play of his own in performance . . . at least he could see for himself the effects of the play on successive audiences and go back to his desk for another attempt feeling that he had made some sort of touch with the realities of theatrical production.'

It was pointed out that the costs of West End productions were too high to try new authors, and, hence, they became frustrated:

'The prospect of English dramatic authorship could hardly be darker; yet this very Easter gilds them with a ray of hope as bright as it is solitary . . . and despairing young playwrights must have rubbed their eyes in astonishment when they read what are to be the aims of the new enterprise.'[6]

*Plays and Players* added:

'Such is the enthusiasm of the new company that it promises to be one of the most vital on the West End scene for many years . . . George Devine, with his past association with Michel Saint-Denis and the Young Vic, is the ideal choice for leading this new venture.'[7]

Following the announcement in the Kingsway, the press covered every new development of the English Stage Company. One of those developments might have ended the venture before it began: after more thorough surveying of the Kingsway, it became clear that it would be impossible to renovate that theatre for less than £150,000. That sum was totally out of the question. Neville Blond, at Alfred Esdaile's suggestion, began negotiations for the lease of the Royal Court Theatre in Sloane Square.

Although not located within the main theatre district of the West End, as was the Kingsway, the Royal Court had other advantages. It, too, had been damaged by bombs during the Second World War. It had stood unused until Alfred Esdaile and the London Theatre Guild Ltd bought it in 1952. Esdaile had at first tried to run the Court as a club theatre, with Lewenstein as manager, but with little success. After about six months, it was decided to close down and do the repairs necessary to get a public licence. The Court had opened

several months later with all regulations met and enough re-
decoration for it to be attractive. So, the theatre had the advantage of
being ready for use with very few additional alterations needed. It
also had the advantage of its history. In 1887 improvements to
Sloane Square were made and the previous Royal Court Theatre, a
converted chapel, was demolished. The present building, designed
by Walter Emlen and W. R. Crewe, was opened on 24 September
1888.

The main successes of the early period were provided by Pinero
farces, but in 1903 J. H. Leigh took over the management of the
theatre and produced a season of Shakespearean revivals. J. E.
Vedrenne joined Leigh for the last of these, *The Two Gentlemen of
Verona*, and Harley Granville-Barker, long associated with the
English Stage Society, produced. Vedrenne and Granville-Barker
persuaded Leigh to allow them to present special matinées of George
Bernard Shaw's *Candida* and from this came the famous Vedrenne-
Barker seasons which were to revolutionize the theatre in England.
In two-and-a-half years, from the middle of 1904 until 1907, thirty-
two plays were presented, representing the work of seventeen
playwrights, many of them thought uncommercial before their
chance at the Court. Certainly Shaw was made popular through the
production there of eleven of his plays – including *Candida, John
Bull's Other Island, Man and Superman, Major Barbara, Captain
Brassbound's Conversion, The Doctor's Dilemma,* and *You Never
Can Tell.* Other playwrights who were given a showing included
Ibsen, Galsworthy, Gerhart Hauptman, John Masefield, Maurice
Maeterlinck, and Gilbert Murray's translations of Euripides. The
Royal Court under the Vedrenne-Barker management also sought to
change the stiff, forced acting style of the day. The new drama
required a more naturalistic style of production and ensemble acting.
These same problems were to be faced fifty years later by the English
Stage Company.

Another important period at the Court began in 1924 when Barry
Jackson, with the Birmingham Repertory Company, began his
tenancy with Shaw's *Back to Methuselah*, presented over a period of
five nights, one part each night. Another noteworthy first at the
Court during Jackson's tenancy was the production of Elmer Rice's
*The Adding Machine* in 1928. After several more seasons of Shaw,
the theatre closed for two years and was eventually sold and used as a
cinema until the blitz in 1940, when it closed again until purchased
by Esdaile.

When the English Stage Company was in the formation stage, the
Court was occupied by Laurier Lister's production of the revue *Airs
on a Shoestring*, which ran for 772 performances. Esdaile was, quite
naturally, loath to give up the theatre. But by the time Blond approached him with the proposition that the English Stage Company
acquire the lease – saying, 'We can replace that; we're on a
shoestring ourselves' – the Royal Court was again having little
success. Esdaile agreed to cancel the English Stage Company's contract for the Kingsway – which, at any rate, was occupying land very
valuable as an office site – and sold them the lease on the Royal
Court, which had thirty-five years to run.

Thus, in November 1955, the English Stage Company was able to announce that it had taken the historic Royal Court. At last a permanent and significant home had been found and planning for the first season was able to get underway.

Part of the plans for developing a style in production and design called for a permanent cyclorama. This surround was called for both as an ideal and as a necessity. It was a necessity because production costs had to be kept at a minimum — only £2,000 was budgeted for each production and that was to include not only décor, but also artists' salaries, props, wardrobe materials and wages, electrical and films, recordings and sound, photos, scripts, cartage, and all the miscellaneous overtime, hires, travel, and dozens of small expenses which occur in any production before opening night. Design and décor, under such limited financial resources, had to be kept simple. But, besides necessity, and perhaps more important, was the ideal. The Royal Court was founded primarily as a writers' theatre. The author has always come first. This didn't mean, of course, that there would be shoddy productions. Quite the contrary: it has always been felt that justice to the script can only be served by good décor. But the décor was never meant to overshadow the script, to steal from its effectiveness or to distract from its faults. Further, by keeping production costs at a minimum, the right to fail has been well served. A doubtful play cannot be produced if the initial expense is enormous, thus demanding a high box office return; and even with 'less doubtful' plays, the script remains central.

It would also seem that in the area of décor Copeau's influence, through his nephew Michel Saint-Denis, was again being felt. Copeau's Vieux-Colombier, also dedicated to reinstating the playscript to a position of primacy, had instituted basic reforms in scenic design, which he simplified to the point of symbolism. His stage had a fixed setting, and locations and atmosphere were indicated by props, screens, small set-pieces, and lighting. The same permanent-set idea was basic to Saint-Denis's idea for the Old Vic Theatre Centre and central to the philosophy of that project. It seems reasonable to assume that George Devine, a disciple and close friend of Saint-Denis, followed the same line of thought when plans for the Royal Court stage were being drawn up. Jocelyn Herbert had had to drop out of the project, so the new permanent setting was designed by Percy Harris of the Motley design company.

The permanent acting company was gathered and when finally complete included John Welsh, Joan Plowright, Ann Morrish, Christopher Felts, Marcia Manolescou, Connie Smith, Alan Bates, Nigel Davenport, Stephen Dartnell, Robert Stephens and George Selway. In addition, Peggy Ashcroft, Gwen Ffrangcon-Davies, Michael Gwynne, Mary Ure and Keith Michell agreed to perform for more limited periods than the others.

On 27 January 1956, the cash balance of the Company was overdrawn by £172 14s. As a result of a contribution of £3,000 from Neville Blond and advance bookings for *The Threepenny Opera*, the balance on 7 February had been brought up to £3,076 19s. Mr Esdaile at that point said he would loan the company £1,000 in four instalments of £250 each and Lord Harewood had signed his form of guarantee for £1,000. Sir Reginald Kennedy-Cox also wrote to say that the Company would receive his donation of £2,000.

The Honorary Secretary ('Honorary' because the position carried no salary), Greville Poke, also reported that George Devine had made a generous gesture to the Company by refusing to accept his full salary as from 19 December 1955, the date of his official appointment as Artistic Director, to the opening date of the first production. Devine had made it clear that he could ill afford such a cut, but he had felt that he would like to do it as a contribution towards the work to be done. Tony Richardson had also taken a salary cut, for the same reasons, as of 9 January 1956, the date of his appointment, to the date of the first production.

With the organization established, the theatre taken, the new stage under construction, and Neville Blond looking after the finances, it was necessary for 'the artistic boys', as Blond called them, to find the plays to be presented the first season. An advertisement seeking new scripts was placed in *The Stage*, the weekly theatre newspaper, and novelists were approached and encouraged to try writing for the theatre. On 2 March 1956, the first five plays of the new season were announced.

## Notes

1. Ivor Brown, *Theatre 1954–5*, Max Reinhardt, 1955, p. 9.
2. 'A Writer's Theatre,' *New Statesman and Nation,* 24 March 1956, p. 272.
3. Michel Saint-Denis, *Theatre: The Rediscovery of Style*, Heinemann Education Books, Ltd, 1960, p. 92.
4. 'Nursery for the Drama,' *Plays and Players,* March 1956, p. 3.
5. *Ten Years at the Royal Court, 1955–1966*, The English Stage Company, p. 1.
6. *The Times,* 31 March 1956.
7. *Plays and Players*, September 1955, p. 20.

# 2 In Operation-the First Season

On 2 April 1956, Angus Wilson's *The Mulberry Bush* was presented at the Royal Court Theatre as the first production of the English Stage Company. Although the production, directed by George Devine, was generally praised, to say that the play was an instant success would be far from accurate.

*The Mulberry Bush* is very nearly a well-made play and it shares both the strengths and weaknesses of that genre. As Eric Rhode puts it: 'Like James and Shaw, Wilson ennobles the form with his witty and percipient dialogue; but at the same time, the formula traps him and he is unable to present in any immediate sense the reality which his characters deny.'[1] A serious attack on 'do-gooders' who are so much out of touch with the reality around them and so insensitive to the feelings of those with whom they deal that they cause irreparable pain, the play sometimes sinks under the weight of its theme. The symbol of the mulberry bush, around which the characters symbolically dance while hurling their barbs at one another, is inadequate to the point of often becoming an obstructive gimmick.

The critics gave the play a 'mixed reception'. The *Liverpool Daily Post* called it 'an intelligent play', but commented that only the actress Agnes Lauchlan saved it from 'the edge of excessive solemnity'. The *Daily Sketch* headlined: 'Mulberry Bush Gets So Boring.' While conceding the play's strong points – its development of atmosphere and sometimes-witty dialogue – it pointed out that Wilson 'doesn't yet know how to make melodramatic passages plausible – nor how to save his characters from becoming irritating bores.' It then said, 'I hope Lord Harewood and his colleagues will choose more discerningly.' The *Daily Express*, on the other hand, said, 'Here is a play which breaks new ground, full of vital characters . . . The new venture looks like a success.' *The Times* called it 'a novelist's play, reading somewhat better than it acts', but also thought it well worth seeing. The *Daily Mail,* while calling it a 'bad play, underdeveloped and overwritten', went on to say, 'but I wish there were more bad plays as fundamentally good – and I dearly hope Mr Wilson's first will not be his last.' The general attitude of all the critics, however, was very nicely summed up by Alan Dent in the *News Chronicle*:

'You will be very foolish – foolisher than ever – if you miss seeing *The Mulberry Bush* . . . because it has had what is called a mixed reception from the critics. The immediate and urgent point is that this is the first production of the English Stage Company

17

... and ought surely to be encouraged if the live theatre is to survive at all.'

And the *Tribune* expressed the point exactly when it said:

> '*The Mulberry Bush*, of course, has many flaws: *it is, after all, Mr Wilson's first play* [my italics]. But the important thing is that he – and many writers like him – should be given the chance to learn by experience, and to go on learning; and this can only be supplied in London by a theatre like the Royal Court.'

And that is exactly why *The Mulberry Bush* was chosen as the opening production: it was, and has remained, the English Stage Company's policy that writers should be given the chance to learn the craft of playwriting by experience and to go on learning. *The Mulberry Bush* had already been produced, unsuccessfully, at the Bristol Old Vic in October 1955 but had been extensively revised since then. It thus satisfied the requisites of being a new play by a successful novelist who had not written for theatre before, and who, it was hoped, would learn from the production and would continue to write for theatre. Wilson himself said:

> 'One hour spent in rehearsal teaches a writer more about playwriting than a month of working in isolation ... The fantastic economics of the West End theatre make this essential learn-as-you-write process impossible ... The Royal Court scheme for presenting new English plays should attract established novelists, for it will give them the opportunity to learn the new craft and attain the London production that must be their goal and their just reward.'[2]

Devine wanted the dramatists to look upon the Court as a workshop and invited them to attend any rehearsals, not only of their own plays, but also of other people's. Another implementation of that policy was the informal Saturday get-togethers in which aspiring and practising playwrights and directors discussed their problems and exchanged ideas.

On 9 April, Arthur Miller's *The Crucible*, also directed by Devine, was added to the repertoire. First produced in America in 1952, this highly effective drama of the Salem witch-hunts, set in seventeenth-century Massachusetts, met with great critical success. It, too, had been seen at the Bristol Old Vic in November 1954 but had met with little success there. The Royal Court's production, again in the permanent setting and using only suggestive pieces and lighting to delineate locale, was called by Richard Findlater of *Tribune* 'one of the most exciting dramas to be staged in London this decade.' *The Times* called it 'a work of art', and went on to say, 'in its economy of means, its bareness, its power to create dramatic effect by dramatic methods, it puts every living English playwright to shame.' Although a success with the critics, *The Crucible* played to only forty-five per cent of box office capacity – the same as *The Mulberry Bush* had achieved. The Council had based their budgets on a cautious fifty per cent of financial capacity, thus allowing plays to continue in performance with far less than the normal seventy-five to eighty-five per cent of capacity required by the commercial managements. However, the audience, in spite of encouragement and prodding by the critics, was not responding to even this minimal requirement.

On 8 May 1956, the English Stage Company added a third play to its repertoire: *Look Back in Anger*, by a young little-known actor, John Osborne. Although the results from the advertisement in the *Stage* had been generally disappointing – Duncan and Devine both admitted that very few of the 675 plays submitted were worth more than a glance – *Look Back in Anger* had been one of those. Duncan was sufficiently impressed after reading it that he immediately sent a telegram to Osborne congratulating him, and the Artistic Committee readily agreed with Devine that here was a play which answered all the requisites of the English Stage Company.

Osborne, who had been acting in a provincial repertory company, had no job and no money. He was hired by the Court and appeared in several productions while his own play was being established. For it is not true that *Look Back in Anger* was an immediate success.

On the other hand, the popular myth that its merits were overlooked by all except Kenneth Tynan, then critic for the *Observer*, is not true either. In fact, the *News Chronicle* called it 'an interesting, but less than successful offering', but did point out that 'it is at least noteworthy for attempting to say *something* about contemporary life.' *The Times* found passages of 'good violent writing', but found it 'squalid' and 'totally inadequate'. Derek Granger of the *Financial Times*, calling it 'this arresting, painful and sometimes astonishing first play', saw both the faults and the promise:

'Its terms are always shrill and sometimes affected ... Mr Osborne communicates no sense to us that he has taken even three paces back from the work that has so hotly and tormentedly engaged him. But for all that it is a play of extraordinary importance.'

Cecil Wilson of the *Daily Mail*, proclaiming Osborne 'a great writer', said:

'They have not discovered a great masterpiece, but *have* discovered a dramatist of outstanding promise: a man who can write with a searing passion, but happens in this case to have lavished it on the wrong play.'

That *Look Back in Anger* was a tremendous breakthrough into the middle-class middle-age preserve of theatre was certainly appreciated by John Barker, critic for the *Daily Express*: 'It is intense, angry, feverish, undisciplined. It is even crazy. But it is young, young, young.' Harold Conway of the *Daily Sketch* had the same reaction:

'John Osborne is a twenty-seven-year-old actor, until recently unemployed, who believes his generation has been given a raw deal.

So he has written a play on the subject. That it turned out last night the most exaggerating play I've seen for years doesn't alter an important fact: Mr Osborne is a new dramatist of importance.'

Milton Shulman of the *Evening Standard* lashed the play and its theme unmercifully, but then said:

> 'But beneath the rasping, negative whine of this play one can distinguish the considerable promise of its author. Mr John Osborne has a dazzling aptitude for provoking and stimulating dialogue, and he draws characters with firm, convincing strokes. When he stops being angry – or lets us in on what he is angry about – he may write a very good play.'

Robert Wraight of the *Star* concurred:

> 'There are enough clever lines in this first play by ... John Osborne to keep a more experienced playwright for life ... In *Look Back in Anger*, Mr Osborne rakes a muckheap with a talent of an immature Tennessee Williams and wraps up his findings in a virtuoso display of passionate overwriting that makes us look forward in high hope to his next play.'

Although not pleased with the play, the *Manchester Guardian* reviewer, Philip Hope-Wallace, did think it had 'enough tension, feeling and originality of theme to make the choice understandable ... it must have wakened echoes in anyone who has not forgotten the frustrations of youth.' He called it a 'muddled first drama', but continued, 'But I believe they have got a potential playwright at last, all the same.' The *Glasgow Herald* saw no good in *Look Back in Anger* or in John Osborne: 'Let us by all means encourage new playwrights if they are good, but not just because they are new – and I cannot see much else in favour of this one at the moment.' In direct opposition to the *Glasgow Herald*, the influential Harold Hobson of the *Sunday Times* wrote of Osborne: 'Though the blinkers still obscure his vision, he is a writer of outstanding promise, and the English Stage Company is to be congratulated on having discovered him.' Alex Matheson Cain of the *Tablet*, the Catholic weekly, said:

> 'A new author in the West End theatre is always an excitement, and whatever the merits of John Osborne's *Look Back in Anger* ... it cannot be denied that this is the sort of play of which we ought to have as much as possible.'

The importance of the play was not lost on the *New Statesman and Nation*, either:

> 'Of course, *Look Back in Anger* is not a perfect play. But it is a most exciting one, abounding with life and vitality, and the life it deals with is life as it is lived at this very moment – not a common enough subject in the English Theatre ... If you are young, it will speak for you. If you are middle-aged, it will tell you what the young are feeling.'

The critical assessment went on and on throughout the summer and, with the eventual tour, into the following year. Some liked the play, some damned it; but very few were blind to either its strong points or the promise of its author.

However, it was indeed Kenneth Tynan of the *Observer* who created the most excitement with his famous summation of its importance:

> 'That the play needs changes I do not deny: it is twenty minutes too long, and not even Mr Haigh's bravura could blind me to the painful whimsy of the final reconciliation scene. I agree that *Look Back in Anger* is likely to remain a minority taste. What matters, however, is the size of the minority. I estimate it at roughly 6,733,000, which is the number of people in this country between the ages of twenty and thirty ... I doubt if I could love anyone who did not wish to see *Look Back in Anger*. It is the best young play of its decade.'

Again, in spite of the tremendous critical enthusiasm, the play was not financially successful during its first run in repertory at the Court. The five-shilling seats were sold, but the percentage of financial capacity was very low indeed. However, Osborne was a success. He had enough offers to keep him busy for five years. *Look Back in Anger* was being considered for a film, and he had already earned enough money to pay his first income tax ever. The English Stage Company purchased the rights of first refusal on Osborne's next three plays for £50, and on 3 July it was decided to purchase the United States rights of *Look Back in Anger* for £200 in advance of royalties. By obtaining these rights the Company would be able to present the play in the United States or sell it to another management. If a production were staged in the United States, the Company would also obtain an additional twenty-five per cent of the film rights, if any. Several tentative offers were received during the summer for a Broadway production, but none of them was firm or entirely satisfactory. Oscar Lewenstein, as General Manager of the Company, was in constant negotiations for a New York production throughout the year. On 3 July the Company's United States rights lapsed, but Osborne agreed to extend them, and, in February 1957, after it had had a successful run in the autumn, word was received that David Merrick was definitely interested, and it was agreed on 12 April that Merrick would produce *Look Back in Anger* in New York the following September after a two-week tryout tour. By the time New York finally saw *Look Back in Anger*, it had toured in England and Osborne had had another hit at the Court.

On 14 May, Ronald Duncan's two poetic verse plays, *Don Juan* and *The Death of Satan*, were added to the repertoire. Originally presented separately as full-length plays at the Devon Festival in 1953 and 1954, they had been cut down, at George Devine's request, so that they could both be performed in one evening.

When Sir Reginald Kennedy-Cox subscribed £2,000 to the English Stage Company, it was with the stipulation that these two plays be produced and that George Selway, a young actor in whom

Kennedy-Cox was interested, should be cast in them. Although this latter proviso was as embarrassing to Duncan and Selway as it was to Devine, Duncan further claims that Devine's lack of enthusiasm for the plays themselves was 'absolutely lethal'; and Tony Richardson admits that they considered the production of *Don Juan* and *The Death of Satan* as paying their 'pound of flesh'.

The extremes of vice and virtue and the modern trend of hovering lukewarmly between those extremes is the subject of *The Death of Satan*. The play opens in a hell where everyone is bored, but reasonably happy, suffering no sense of deprivation. Shaw, Oscar Wilde and Lord Byron while away their *ennui* by playing poker with the Ten Commandments as their counters, occasionally enlivening the game by gambling their literary reputations. Wilde wagers *Lady Windermere's Fan*; Shaw raises the stake with *Mrs Warren's Profession*. Satan, unable to understand why his visitors no longer suffer in hell, sends Don Juan back to earth to investigate. Don Juan reports back that no one can suffer any more because, loving nothing, they have nothing to lose. So Satan, his purpose in after-life having been destroyed, dies. The play is written as a satire against a mediocre age in which no one either believes or disbelieves and can therefore feel no remorse.

*Don Juan* takes the position that the historic seducer was by no means a cynical profligate who invited his own destruction, but a man who led his life in search of true love as an attempt to recover from unrequited love.

Although Duncan claims that Devine deliberately sabotaged the plays, that certainly cannot be proved.

It had been suggested by Duncan that the two plays be produced in their full-length versions and played back-to-back in repertory. Not only did Devine not like the plays, but he also thought it a terrible financial risk to play them both in repertory at that point – for the Company's only financial support was Neville Blond. Blond would tell the members of the Management Committee, 'Don't worry. We'll be alright for money, but don't tell the artistic boys.' Devine didn't know quite how the Company was standing financially and felt he was right in his concern. His drastic cutting of the two plays to form one, however, was a mistake, judging from the critics' reactions. Almost without exception the long four-hour performance which resulted was unfavourably commented upon. Duncan's concern, however, was more with the artistic result than simply with the length of playing time. He felt that Devine had cut his plays to shreds, had slashed the texts to a skeleton of stage directions so that they were reduced to a long costume melodrama. The critics generally reflected that view. Milton Shulman, in a crushing review in the *Evening Standard*, called the plays 'a dustbin of barren ideas', and found 'neither the poetry significant enough nor the philosophy profound enough to justify so devious a route to reach so humdrum a conclusion.' But even Shulman pointed out that 'Mr Duncan has occasional moments of amusing cynicism and an above-average ration of wit.' Most reviewers, though generally unfavourable in their reception of the evening, were not so harsh; but it was generally agreed that of the two, *The Death of Satan* was by far the better.

Harold Hobson said that he 'did not think much of *Don Juan* when I saw it some time ago at a Taw and Torridge Festival; and my opinion of it in itself is not improved', but he did think *The Death of Satan* 'brilliant'. The *Stage*, on the other hand, blazoned, 'Ronald Duncan's two Don Juan plays . . . must be counted among the most interesting and best written of the season.' The *Stage*, unfortunately, was far and away in the minority.

Again, Duncan claims that after cutting his texts to shreds, Devine's 'next move was to sabotage my intentions by inspired miscasting . . . For Don Juan he found an actor who had rightly found his place in musical comedy, for Doña Aña a lady who would have made an adequate Mother Courage, and for the frivolous and amorous Isabella, an actress who might have passed as an officer of a Marriage Guidance Clinic.' He does go on to say, 'It is fair to say that Devine handled the technical problems which the plays contain, such as the ghost scene, with more than average competence. I could not fault the surgeon though he was removing my guts and heart.'[3] The critics, however, generally found good to say of both the production and the cast. But their reception of the plays was far from flattering and there was reason for Duncan saying, 'Bent over Sloane Square with my trousers down, I received a beating of expletives.'

Although Duncan's analysis of Devine's motivations is certainly questionable, his depiction of the results is not. Devine admitted that he had hurt the plays' chances by cutting them so extensively. At a party at Lord Harewood's after the opening-night performance, Patricia Lawrence, Greville Poke's wife, found Devine sitting alone looking miserable and on the verge of tears. Although he hadn't talked to any of the critics, he knew what their reactions would be, and he said, 'I shouldn't have done it. I should have let someone else direct them who was more sympathetic to them. It was a great mistake and it was all my fault.'

It is unthinkable that George Devine would ever have deliberately sabotaged another artist's work, but it is true that he felt he was performing a contractual obligation, that he probably communicated that feeling to the cast, and that he was out of sympathy with Duncan's poetic plays.

For the fact is, the poetic drama revival which began with Eliot's *Murder in the Cathedral* in 1935 had already reached its culmination with Duncan's *This Way to the Tomb* in 1947 and the Eliot and Fry plays of the early 1950s. Devine felt – and the evidence supports that he felt rightly – that the drama was moving in new directions, that more poetry could be found in the prose plays of Osborne than in the verse plays of Duncan.

Duncan was, and is, understandably bitter. He says, 'I had laboured hard towards this fiasco. I had eaten my way through dozens of terrible meals to form the English Stage Company. I had suffered the company of bores, pandars, pimps, and profiteers.'[4] He had founded a company to revitalize the drama and then was told that that company found the vitality of drama in areas other than his own.

But it would be wrong to dismiss Ronald Duncan as a poet-dramatist who founded an organization just so that his own plays

could be produced. It must be remembered that he did recognize the
value of *Waiting for Godot* and tried to get it produced; that he did
recognize the value of *The Threepenny Opera*, put his own money on
it, and tried to have it produced; that he was, in fact, instrumental in
reintroducing Brecht into England after the Second World War and
was ahead of the later rage for Brecht; and that he did like *Look Back
in Anger* and praised Osborne for it. He did, of course, hope that the
English Stage Company would provide a new outlet for the verse
drama of which he had been so much a part and which he considered
the new hope in a stagnant field. It cannot be denied that Duncan
was, as John Osborne put it, 'used badly'. But the new wave of drama
which was to issue from the Royal Court was to be far different from
that which Duncan had envisaged and the revolutionary management started by Duncan was to produce a dramatic revolution far
beyond what he had anticipated.

On 26 June 1956, the fourth production was added to the repertoire — *Cards of Identity*, a satirical fantasy by novelist Nigel Dennis. Commissioned by George Devine after reading Dennis's novel of
the same name, it is a satire on contemporary snobbishness illu-
strating that society is able to change any individual's identity to suit
its purpose, that we are only a mass of conditioned reflexes which can
easily be manipulated, thus allowing the 'people upstairs' to do with
us what they will and to take from us whatever they want. Dennis
used techniques which, easily judged in retrospect, were ahead of
their time. Robert Kee of the *Daily Mirror*, after saying the play was
'brilliantly written', lamented, 'Unfortunately it was also weird, con-
fusing, and difficult to follow.' The general critical reaction was one
of confusion. However, Richard Findlater, in his perceptive,
exuberant review, saw it as another indication of the revival of
theatre:

> '*Cards of Identity* . . . will probably lose the Company's excellent
> sponsors a bit more money, but it is exactly the kind of play which
> the Royal Court ought to put on and it is a kind of play which the
> English theatre needs . . .
> 'For *Cards of Identity* is not only important for its content, but
> for its form: it demonstrates what you can and cannot do inside
> the picture-frame stage, how far you can go with the old-
> fashioned novelties of dramatic inset and actors' cartoons, and . . .
> how much is lost in the well-made play that the inexpert novelist
> can recapture for the stage providing that he is given his head.'

Other critics were more interested in picking at the flaws than in
pointing to the virtues. Harold Hobson, though, found it 'altogether
an evening of idiosyncratic and bewildering pleasure and
excitement.' *Universe*, the Catholic weekly, certainly reflected a part
of the audience reaction: 'The peculiarly modern blasphemy of the
violation of men's souls, the changing of personalities by psychiatric
treatment, is the theme of a loathsome play at the Royal Court
Theatre, *Card of Identity*.'

Three months after opening, the English Stage Company had five
plays in its repertoire – two by established English novelists in their

forties, one by an American playwright, two by an established poet-dramatist, and one by an English actor in his twenties. But for the first nine weeks the audiences had not filled even the budgeted fifty per cent of financial capacity. *The Mulberry Bush* never really caught the public's attention; *The Crucible* seemed to start well, but interest fell with the introduction into the repertory of *Look Back in Anger*; and *Look Back in Anger* – though certainly arousing controversy – also failed to attract audiences at first. Then, in a meeting to discuss the fate of *Anger*, George Fearon, the Company press officer, suggested the 'angry young man' theme. He followed up with press releases using that now well-known phrase and it excited the public interest. Receipts immediately rose to about sixty per cent of capacity. The Duncan plays had had to be withdrawn after only eight performances at twenty-two per cent of financial capacity. *Cards of Identity* had aroused interest, but, although fifty-seven per cent of the seating capacity was sold, the box office takings averaged only forty-six per cent, just below the break-even level. The total box office loss after three months was over £8,000.

This lack of attendance was partly attributable to the fact that, strange as it seems today, the audiences weren't used to plays being done in repertory. Now, with the National Theatre and the Aldwych, people have become accustomed to having different plays on alternating nights, but in 1956 they were confused by this and found it hard to know what was going on on a particular night. To help overcome this it was decided in May that rather than putting a new play on to run for three days and then taking it off, to be re-presented a week or ten days later, the new play would run a week, be replaced for three days of the following week, and then played again for the last three days of that second week. That policy was adopted and seemed to have some effect, but audiences still remained somewhat confused about which play was being given on a particular night. An 'audience organizer' was hired to arrange parties to attend the theatre. Although he sold £71 worth of block bookings in two weeks, it was decided by the end of the summer to do away with the position as essentially unprofitable.

*The Good Woman of Setzuan*, with Peggy Ashcroft as the lead, was scheduled to open at the Court on 31 October to run for six uninterrupted weeks, after a week in Brighton and a week in Oxford. The pre-Court presentations were meant to initiate the English Stage Company's policy of enlivening theatre in the provinces as well as in London. It was not meant as a try-out tour. The Company was faced in early July with deciding what should be presented until the Brecht commitment. *The Crucible, The Mulberry Bush* and the Duncan plays had had to be withdrawn, leaving *Look Back in Anger* and *Cards of Identity* playing. Eventually it was decided that *Look Back in Anger* would be allowed to run alone for eleven weeks, more as an act of faith than as evidence of a real belief that it would pay for itself. By mid-September the Council was giving earnest consideration to whether *Look Back in Anger* should be taken off three weeks before the end of its allotted run, which would mean putting in another production, or whether it should be kept on until the opening of *The Good Woman of Setzuan*. It was not covering its expenses

and a twenty-five minute excerpt had already been sold to the B.B.C.
for televising on 16 October. This, it was feared, would fulfil any
curiosity the potential audience might have and would be death at
the box office. Neville Blond, however, maintained that the television
broadcast, instead of killing interest, would actually arouse it.
Although he was certainly the minority in his view, he felt so strongly
that he was right that he finally said he would guarantee the Company against any loss which *Look Back in Anger* might incur after 16
October. He was proved right. The critics warned their readers for
days before the event to be sure to see the excerpt and, after the
broadcast, praised it highly and asked, 'When can we see the entire
play, please?' The audience provided the answer themselves: within
three days four sacks of letters requesting tickets had been received.
The play that had caused so much talk and critical excitement had
finally become a box office hit as well. With only three weeks left to
run before *The Good Woman of Setzuan* commitment forced it off
the stage, the English Stage Company – as has so often happened –
was unable to exploit its hard-won success to the full. On 5
November, *Look Back in Anger* was transferred to the Lyric
Theatre, Hammersmith, where it continued to play to full houses for
another three weeks before it again had to be withdrawn because that
theatre had been previously committed. Though there was some
faint interest expressed, it was not transferred into the West End until 1968, after it had again been revived at the Royal Court.

*The Good Woman of Setzuan* had a successful tour and opened at
the Royal Court on 31 October 1956. Although Kenneth Tynan,
since 1954, had certainly tried to pave the way by his championship
of Brecht, and the Berliner Ensemble had visited London for the first
time in August and September of 1956, neither the play nor the
production was well received. In a shattering, condescending review,
Harold Hobson of the *Sunday Times* summed up the negative reaction to Brecht:

'Thus he [Brecht] tells the tale of the good woman of Setzuan in a
series of straightforward simplified scenes like those in an in-
fant's schoolbook. In Eric Bentley's excellent translation he
employs a language denuded of any subtlety or overtones. From
time to time he diverts the illiterate audience he is attempting to
reach and convert with songs and with comic [sic] like a woman
pretending to be a man and trying to smoke a cigar . . . I can understand why a young man sitting three rows behind me . . . left at
the first interval; . . . why a young woman not far away, after
valiantly attempting to laugh at the clumsy jokes in the first act,
said to her companion, "I think this is the dullest evening I have
ever spent in a theatre", . . . why the older man sitting next to me
remarked, "Every time the water carrier yawns once, I yawn
twice . . ."

'But though I can understand these people, I cannot agree with
them . . . An audience which goes to the Court theatre and plays
the game properly, which throws away its sophistication, which
abandons its irritation at being told the same thing over and over
again, leaves its intelligence in the cloakroom, and is willing to in-

troduce the mentality of six into bodies of sixteen, twenty-six, or sixty, will have a tolerable time.'

Hobson then eloquently praised the performances and said that 'this production is better than those given by the East Berlin Company . . .' and finished with a few pokes at Osborne the actor and Osborne the playwright, warning him not to be influenced by Brecht's style.[5]

Tynan, on the other hand, rushed to the defence of Brecht, saying that though the style seemed simple, the message – let us change human nature by changing the world – was actually very complicated. It was the production that he found lacking.

'In George Devine's production the great challenge is partly muffed. Honourably bent on directing his cast along cool, detached Brechtian lines, Mr Devine forgets that the Brechtian method works only with team-actors of great technical maturity. With greener players it looks like casual dawdling.'

He found only Devine's acting good and found Eric Bentley's translation 'clumsy'. But, said Tynan, the play 'shouldn't be missed'.

With these stands taken by the two most influential critics and with the rest of the critics essentially aligned with one or other of them, the play was doomed to popular failure. It is surprising that it did as well as it did – fifty-nine per cent of financial capacity sold.

One of the outcomes of *The Good Woman of Setzuan* was the launching of Peggy Ashcroft into modern, non-traditional plays. She was certainly not to be the last great player to find new horizons through acting at the Royal Court.

Wycherley's *The Country Wife*, which opened on 12 December 1956, had been suggested as early as June. The lack of financial success of the early productions had alarmed Neville Blond and he hoped to remedy the situation with this revival. The play was also selected as part of the evolving policy of reviving neglected classics. *The Country Wife* had certainly been produced since Restoration days, but it often raised what now seems a surprising amount of moral indignation. The most famous of these outcries arose over the 1936 production of Tyrone Guthrie at the Old Vic. The press was shocked and letters to *The Times* expressed horror at the depravity of the Old Vic. The English Stage Company's revival was met much more calmly. To be sure, every critic pointed out the bawdiness in rather pristine phrases, but generally took the attitude of *The Times*: 'If we are not squeamish there is much to admire in the sureness of touch with which this ribald comedy is organized.' But there was little real difference of opinion about the production, though some called it 'brilliant' and others thought it merely 'good'. Though the *Daily Mail* 'detected no weakness in the style of this revival', Harold Hobson found most of the Company wanting 'both style and a style'. But, as Hobson also pointed out,'This [lack of style] which would be fatal in Congreve, does little to the tougher, rougher Wycherley.'

*The Country Wife* ran for sixty performances at the Royal Court to 94.8 per cent of seating capacity and ninety per cent of financial capacity. It also provided the English Stage Company with its first transfer into the West End, when Jack Hylton approached the Company with an offer to transfer its production to the Adelphi Theatre at the end of its Royal Court run. The English Stage Company was to pay the artists' salaries, transfer costs, and publicity, all up to an agreed maximum. In return, Mr Hylton agreed to cover the Company's losses, if any, and to guarantee a minimum profit of £500 against fifty-five per cent of the net takings. This meant that the Company could not lose: if the Adelphi took a gross of £2,000 per week, the English Stage Company would make a small extra profit; if the gross were approximately £3,000 per week, the profit to the English Stage Company would amount to £1,000 a week. These figures were dependent upon the Entertainments Tax rebate – fifteen per cent of gross takings. As part of the orginal act, the Treasury, operating through the Commission of Customs and Excise, allowed exemptions from the tax if the entertainment were both of a wholly 'educational' character and not given for profit. Non-profit was defined as 'entertainments the whole takings of which were devoted to charity', but by 1953, primarily because of the difficulty of determining what was 'partly educational', exemptions were granted on the non-profit-distributing constitution of the production organization. The importance of the exemption was, of course, enormous. Although the tax was theoretically paid by the customer and only collected by the theatre management, the public, in effect, refused to pay higher ticket prices, thus placing the tax directly on the management. Thus, the tax represented a great expense – and it applied whether the production proved a flop or a success.

The Arts Council were negotiating with the Commission of Customs and Excise on behalf of the English Stage Company and it was hoped, and finally agreed, that no tax would be paid on the transfer, with that fifteen per cent of the gross to accrue to the Company.[6]

The idea of transferring *The Country Wife* was not at all unusual in England, as it would have been in America at that time. In England, productions which prove profitable in a small theatre, whether a theatre club or a prominent provincial repertory theatre, are often transferred into a West End theatre when it appears that by doing so it can reach a wider audience for a longer time than it could otherwise. The financial arrangements are not always the same – and not always as safe as were those made with Jack Hylton. If an outside management had the rights of a play, they would sometimes just allow the Court to perform the play, sometimes in a joint production with them; sometimes they would just hand over the rights to the Court, but maintain control for further exploitation through transfer, film or television rights, or repertory rights; the outside management might or might not share in the production costs. Sometimes the rights are shared, such as the rights to Osborne's *Hotel in Amsterdam* which were jointly owned by the English Stage Company and Oscar Lewenstein. In that particular case the production costs and transfer costs were shared equally, as were the profits and all the subsidiary rights. The English Stage Company, in other instances, could also transfer its own production without recourse to any outside management.

Although the Royal Court is not a tryout theatre – it does not choose the plays it produces with the main goal of transferring – it did survive through its early years on the profits earned from transfers and the sale of subsidiary rights and continues to depend partly on profits from those sources.

The transfer of *The Country Wife* to the Adelphi Theatre (and later to the Chelsea Palace Theatre) was not without its drawbacks. When the play transferred, it took with it its players. That was one of the causes of the eventual repudiation of the policy of maintaining a permanent acting company.

*The Country Wife* was followed at the Royal Court by Carson McCullers's *Member of the Wedding*, which opened on 5 February 1957. The critics again praised both the play and the production, with the notable exception of Harold Hobson in the *Sunday Times*, who said:

'It has no sense of the economy of art. Most of the sixteen characters suffer from severe underemployment. Miss McCullers does not so much reveal the theme of this play . . . as state it in set terms, in a long speech at the end of the first act . . . I quickly wearied of Frankie Addams's particular psychological problem (whatever that was), and her morbid desire to be one of a crowd.'

Hobson's colleague on *The Times* disagreed with him:

'The theme is the sense of "not belonging". Miss McCullers draws a firm contrast between the spectacular workings of the sense in the despair that may overwhelm adolescence round the age of twelve and the unspectacular acceptance by an adult, of a loneliness born not so much of personal as of racial tensions . . .'

Kenneth Tynan essentially agreed, calling *Member of the Wedding* 'not so much a play as a tone-poem for three voices in two colours, black and white.' Although that would not ordinarily be a favourable recommendation, Tynan continued:

'Miss McCullers bears a charmed style, and wields it like a magic wand . . . Miss McCullers triumphs, partly because her innate tact rejects the phony-primitive, and partly because she is writing about the South . . . The territory is swampy and clodhoppers broach it at their peril. Miss McCullers treads it with apt lightness.'

So again, the Court had a highly praised new play,[7] but despite the critical praise and the televising of an excerpt on B.B.C. on 18 February, the box office did not reflect a success. *Member of the Wedding* played to only thirty-nine per cent of financial capacity and was replaced on 11 March with the first revival of *Look Back in Anger*, which played until 1 April 1957, ending the first year of productions by the English Stage Company.

That first year's programme was to be fairly representative. There had been four productions with decidedly favourable critical acclaim

and four with predominantly unfavourable critical reception. There
had been three imports of plays new to London, five new plays – one
by an unknown actor, two by established novelists, and two by an
already-successful playwright; and there had been one revival of an
English classic. On 9 March 1957, the Company was able to give a
party to celebrate the 100th performance of its successful transfer,
*The Country Wife*. And, largely due to the success of that transfer
and the hard-won success of *Look Back in Anger*, the Company
ended its first year with a surplus of £5,245 – including donations
from individuals and business, and the Arts Council grant.

Some of the original hopes had proved unworkable; the permanent
company of actors playing in repertory was one of these. The transfer
had proved the final blow to that idea. With large numbers of the acting company playing for a long run in the West End it was impossible to plan on their being in up-coming productions at the Court. The
permanent acting company had also proved expensive – actors had
to be paid whether or not they were working – and the actors who
were not in a given production found themselves bored with the
whole idea. The repertory system had early proved unworkable,
largely because of the lack of favourable audience response, and had
already been replaced by the limited-run idea in September.

In spite of the attempts of the audience organizer to develop a
regular audience, the attendance pattern remained just as erratic as it
is at any commercial theatre. That can partly be explained by the
choice of plays: the audience who went to see *The Country Wife*
would have gone to see it anywhere; they were not the same audience
who went to see *Look Back in Anger* or *The Good Woman of Setzuan*. Precisely because of the eclecticism in its choice of plays, the
Royal Court has never been able to develop a faithful audience which
will go to see any new production there – although it has continued to
try.

Another of the original ideas, the permanent setting, was also on
the way out by the end of the first season. It was proving too cumber-
some for the small stage; it didn't allow enough flexibility. Although
George Devine attempted to use the permanent set, Tony Richardson, a man of very powerful personality and determination, didn't
like it and it was largely through his influence that it eventually dis-
appeared. It was used for *The Mulberry Bush, The Crucible, Don
Juan* and *The Death of Satan, The Country Wife, Cards of Identity,*
and *The Good Woman of Setzuan*, but most of it was lost for *Look
back in Anger* and *Member of the Wedding*, both directed by
Richardson. In the second season, the *Fin de Partie* set was brought
from Paris; the surround was vaguely used for *The Entertainer; The
Apollo de Bellac* was completely without the permanent set, and *The
Chairs* had to have a cyclorama. By *The Making of Moo* and
*Nekrassov*, the permanent set was completely gone. However,
although the original idea was lost, most productions – not all of
them – have tended to use elements rather than big sets. There isn't
the space at the Court for big sets: one set can't be brought on while
another is taken off. So the shape of the theatre very much conditions
the kind of designing.

By April 1957, the fame of the English Stage Company had spread.

Ian Hunter, a director of Harold Holt, Artists' Agents, had been approached by the Argentine Government to send a company to Argentina in two years time, all expenses to be guaranteed by the Argentine Government. He approached the English Stage Company with the offer. Although the tour was in fact never carried out, the offer was indicative of the prestigious position which the Company had already achieved. Another offer for a foreign tour, this time for a week's performance of *Look Back in Anger* in Zurich, was also received and accepted. An offer to produce Sartre's *Nekrassov* at the 1957 Edinburgh Festival was accepted. *Look Back in Anger*, though not transferred into the West End, was set for a New York production, and Lewenstein and Mankowitz Productions were taking it to the Youth Festival in Moscow that summer. A request had also been received from Cecil Williams for a lease to present *Look Back in Anger* in South Africa, for which the English Stage Company received ten per cent of the gross, of which John Osborne received two-thirds.

The leasing of rights, the sale of film rights, and profits from successful transfers were to allow the Company to continue operations for many years, in spite of the small Arts Council grants and the inevitable box office deficit. The Royal Court is too small to be successful commercially under the limited-run policy of the English Stage Company. In 1956 the seating capacity of 439 was able to gross only £265 5s 6d. at 100 per cent capacity, with the ticket prices ranging from fifteen shillings to five shillings. While that financial capacity would allow a profit over running costs for most productions, the constant addition of new production costs usually negated any profits. But the budget was based on a more realistic financial taking of fifty per cent of capacity. On that figure the box office would provide an income of roughly £1,000 a week, and running costs for 1957 were budgeted at £1,300 a week, leaving a weekly deficit of £300, or £15,000 for the year. It was decided to ask the Arts Council for half that sum – £7,500 – and the Council members would raise the rest among themselves. The Arts Council, however, responded with only £5,000 for the 1957–8 season, making income from sources other than the box office all the more important.

One persistent problem continued to plague the Company: the lack of worthwhile new British plays. In July 1956, this statement had been read into the minutes of the Management Committee: 'We are receiving and reading plays all the time; one of these may turn out to be presentable.' In January both Neville Blond and Greville Poke had expressed 'serious alarm' that the Company was as yet unable to announce a season of new plays. One of the problems with the plays which were being submitted was that they continued to deal with a society which had passed away, in a language which was dead – the language of upper-class Kensington. (Indeed, one of the attractions of *Look Back in Anger*, apart from its obvious thematic relevance to contemporary life, was its break from the so-called standard English – the English of the Edwardian drawing-room.) So, although over 1,000 new plays had been received, very few had in fact merited production.

By April, though, the first part of the new season was set. The first production was to be the world première of Samuel Beckett's *Fin de Partie* and his *Acte Sans Paroles*, which was to be the first of the English Stage Company's championing of important contemporary French authors – Sartre, Ionesco, Giraudoux, Genet. Again, Devine's interest in the modern French dramatists can be traced to Copeau through Saint-Denis. But Devine had also spent many of his boyhood summers in France with his father and spoke fluent French. And, again, Duncan, who had translated Cocteau and Giraudoux and who had tried so hard to produce Beckett's *Waiting for Godot*, was in favour of producing the French playwrights as a means of inspiring their English colleagues. It was Beckett, though, who made the approach to Devine, who, with the Council's enthusiastic approval, immediately flew to Paris to make production arrangements. It was decided to present the plays at the Royal Court in a French production directed by Roger Blin. The Court agreed to pay production costs, budgeted at £740, and running expenses for one week. As part of the agreement Beckett agreed to translate *Fin de Partie* into English and to give the English Stage Company the option of mounting its own production at a later date, using the original sets. A gala performance was arranged for 3 April 1957, with the French Ambassador to be in attendance. *Fin de Partie* was duly submitted to the Lord Chamberlain's Office for approval and returned in March with one small deletion.

The second production was to be John Osborne's new play, *The Entertainer*. Surprisingly, the inclusion of *The Entertainer* in the new season had caused more trouble than had *Fin de Partie*. The history of *The Entertainer* began early in the run of *Look Back in Anger*.

Sir Laurence Olivier and Marilyn Monroe, who were filming Terence Rattigan's *The Sleeping Prince* together, had gone to see *Look Back in Anger* one night early in its run. Marilyn Monroe liked the play, but Olivier was not terribly impressed. Then Arthur Miller took him to the Court to see the play again and during the course of it Miller said, 'You should get this young man to write a play for you.' John Osborne was there that evening and Olivier saw him during an interval and said, 'Would you write a play for me?' Osborne smiled and said that of course he would. The following day George Devine got Osborne to come to his office and said, 'Larry Olivier's been on the telephone and wants to know when you're going to start writing this play for him.' Osborne was amazed. He had thought Olivier was joking. But with that tremendous encouragement, he started his second play.

That was in the summer of 1956. By 1 March 1957, Sir Laurence Olivier was under contract. The Artistic Committee, which had to approve all of the plays to be produced, had as yet seen only the first act. The second act was given to them then and, a few days later, the final act was finished.

Ronald Duncan disliked the play intensely, thought it a 'bloody flabby play', and said so. Oscar Lewenstein didn't like it either, and with those two opposed to doing it and George Devine very anxious to produce it, the argument was on. Finally, Duncan, Lewenstein, Joe Hodgkinson of the Arts Council, and Greville Poke – who, as

Secretary of the Company, was an *ex officio* member of the Artistic Committee – were invited to lunch at Neville Blond's flat on 7 March. Blond listened to all sides of the argument, and then said, 'I haven't read the play; I don't know what the merits of it are; but I think we ought to do it. For one good reason: John has written *Look Back in Anger*, we've done it; it's his first play for us, and it was rather successful; I think we *owe* it to him to do his second play.'

Greville Poke said, 'I haven't read the play either, Neville, but I think that argument is absolutely unanswerable.'

And it was.

Poke took the play and, after reading it, phoned Blond and said, 'Neville, I don't think you need have any worries about this play; there won't be a dry seat in the house.'

However, there was one point, in particular, which the Committee – especially Poke – felt needed adjustment: the similarity between Mick's death, which is reported in the final act, and the Moorhouse tragedy (in which a young soldier was locked in a closet and suffocated), which took place in fact during the Suez crisis the previous year. It was feared that the newspapers would pick up the parallel and that it would cause unnecessary pain to the boy's parents. Osborne was asked to make that and two smaller changes, but refused, saying that he intended the public to make the connection. It was finally agreed, with Greville Poke dissenting, that Osborne should be approached again on the matter and whether or not he agreed to the alterations the play would be presented.

By 29 March, just ten days after the presentation of *The Entertainer* was announced, the evening performances for the entire fourweek run were sold out. The press never mentioned the Moorhouse–Mick parallel, and the history of the success of *The Entertainer* in the West End, in New York, and as a film is well known.

It is interesting to note that Sir Laurence Olivier – and all the other stars and super-stars who have appeared at the Royal Court under the English Stage Company – received only £30 to £50 a week, although in the West End their salary would range from £700 to £800 a week. This willingness to accept such a tremendous cut in salary is testimony to the greatness of both the stars and the Company.

The Company had been asked in January to present a play for the Devon Festival during the last week of July. After a long search, it was finally decided to produce Oliver Marlow Wilkenson's one act play *How Can We Save Father* and W. B. Yeats's *Purgatory*, with the hopes of transferring them to the Court after the Festival.[8]

It was also decided in March to produce the Dudley Fitts version of *Lysistrata*, but the rights of that translation had already been purchased. Oscar Lewenstein suggested that a new translation could be made for the Royal Court, but Ronald Duncan had just seen the Oxford Repertory Company's production of the Fitts version and was impressed by it. After negotiations, Minos Volonakis, the director of the Oxford Repertory, agreed to direct *Lysistrata* at the Court. The Oxford Repertory wanted to present their production as already scheduled, at Brighton and three other places before going to the Court because they felt the profits would help them to finance their next season. Neville Blond, in view of the sympathetic feeling the

English Stage Company had for the work of the Oxford Repertory
Company, felt that 'we should help them in every way possible', and
the pre-Court tour was agreed upon.

Two more modern French plays were added to the schedule:
Giraudoux's *The Apollo de Bellac*, adapted by Ronald Duncan, and
Ionesco's *The Chairs*, translated by Donald Watson; and the two
novelists-turned-playwright, Angus Wilson and Nigel Dennis, were
working on new plays for the English Stage Company.[9]

The first year had ended with a revival of its most exciting production, and the second year, not yet fully set, already showed promise of
excitement for the world of theatre.

## Notes

1. *Novelists' Theatre*, Introduction by Eric Rhode, Penguin Books,
   1966, p. 15.
2. 'The Novelist in the Theatre,' *Observer*, 18 March 1956.
3. Ronald Duncan, *How to Make Enemies*, Rupert Hart-Davis,
   1968, p. 386.
4. *Ibid.*, p. 387.
5. Osborne, however, was influenced and the result was the dis-
   astrous *World of Paul Slickey* in 1959.
6. Later in 1957 the Entertainments Tax was finally repealed, largely through the effort of A. P. Herbert.
7. Although *Member of the Wedding* had already been filmed, the
   play had not previously been performed in England.
8. *How Can We Save Father* was presented at the Royal Court
   Theatre on 5 August 1957.
9. Dennis's *The Making of Moo* was presented at the Royal Court
   Theatre on 25 June 1957, and either shocked or delighted the
   critics with its satire on organized religion. Angus Wilson's play
   has never been produced.

# 3 1957 to October 1965

In May 1960, as a result of criticism levelled by Ronald Duncan, the aims and objects of the English Stage Company were examined in the light of the past four years' experience and the personalities involved. In a letter prepared for the Council of the English Stage Company, but which got into the hands of the press, Duncan had alleged that the policy had a left-wing bias which permitted second-rate talents with favoured political views to receive production while more noted dramatists who did not share those views were virtually excluded. He charged that social-realistic drama was being presented to the exclusion of other works.

The charge is difficult to defend. By May 1960, the Company had produced fifty-four plays in its main bill and eighteen more new plays for one or two nights each, in all representing the works of fifty-two authors as diverse in their styles and philosophies as Jean-Paul Sartre, Arnold Wesker, Jean Giraudoux, John Osborne, Samuel Beckett, Arthur Miller, Ann Jellicoe, John Arden, Eugène Ionesco, William Wycherley, N. F. Simpson, Georg Büchner, and Harold Pinter. Certainly some of the authors were concerned with social-political problems dealt with in a social-realistic style. Many of the exciting new talents saw and wrote about the world in those terms. But the eclecticism of the plays and authors represented gives little support to the charge that the Royal Court had become the home of left-wing theatre; that it had, in fact, become a new Unity Theatre – a view held by many besides Duncan.

However, Duncan had caused a useful appraisal to be made of the achievements and future aims of the English Stage Company. The Artistic Committee, through its Chairman, Lord Harewood, submitted a document – *Memorandum on Artistic Policy – Aims and Objects* – to the Council, in which they outlined their views of the Company policy and how it should be expanded.

The main objective of the Company remained the same: to promote a consistently progressive policy towards the discovery and development of contemporary dramatists, especially English dramatists. This main objective was not to preclude the presentation of outstanding foreign works 'without which the contemporary scene would be incomplete'; nor did it preclude the classical revival, 'provided that such a production emphasizes some special aspect of performance or style.' While the basic objectives remained the same as originally set out, it was felt that there was room to expand, both in order to discover new talent and to make better use of that which was already centred around the Court. While the Royal Court Theatre would remain as the main platform for the work of the Company, the Artistic Committee proposed four new areas for development:

*A provincial link-up* with one, two, or three provincial repertory theatres: related to the Arts Council 'grid scheme', in which repertory theatres would interchange productions on a weekly basis within a 'grid' of three companies, the scheme would give more outlets for dramatists, and by interchange among the group of theatres – and occasionally with the Royal Court itself – would spread the work of the Company outside London.

*A larger theatre* would allow the Company the possibility of a larger and more popular audience and would enable them to offer a higher proportion of low-priced seats than was possible at the Royal Court. The larger theatre could also lead to the development of a broader form of expression and help to 'open out' the new dramatist in a way which the intimacy of the Royal Court prevents. However, it was also pointed out that while some shows which had been presented at the Court might have been candidates for a larger theatre (*The Country Wife, Lysistrata, Look After Lulu*), the great majority of the work, including such successes as *Look Back in Anger, The Long and The Short and The Tall*, and *Rosmersholm*, would still be presented at the intimate Royal Court. Thus, the larger theatre would not seriously drain the Company's repertoire.

*A studio* for training and development, for a programme of artistic education, was needed by writers, actors and directors if progress in those areas was to be maintained. The Artistic Committee felt that the studio would be an important development in the Company's work.

*Companies of actors* on a semi-permanent, or at least seasonal, basis should be maintained whenever possible.

The Artistic Committee also felt that steps should be taken to enlarge the scope of the Company's audiences, especially to include the untapped young public who rarely set foot inside the Royal Court. But the Committee considered that if the first four objectives were carried out, the widening of the audience would be achieved.

Lest such a programme seem unduly ambitious, the Artistic Committee pointed out that, besides the Artistic Directors – George Devine and Tony Richardson – the Company had a group of six directors – Lindsay Anderson, John Bird, John Blatchley, John Dexter, William Gaskill, and Anthony Page – who could carry out the proposed projects.

Not all the objectives set forth by the Artistic Committee were new. Certainly the basic aim of encouraging and promoting new dramatists was familiar and was the motivation for widening the audience, and attempts to develop a wider audience had been made since the founding of the Company.

One scheme to help create the core of an audience had been announced at the same time that the English Stage Company had proclaimed its existence at the Kingsway Theatre. Originally called the Kingsway Theatre Club, the benefits offered to its members included: (1) exclusive use of the Club lounge and bar for meals; (2) two seats at a reduced rate for all plays produced by the Company in London and in the provinces, whenever possible; (3) advance notice of the Company's productions and priority of booking; (4) at functions with no reserved seats for the general public, such as lectures and films sponsored by the Company, a certain number of seats would be reserved for members only; (5) Sunday performances of plays and films. In return for these benefits, those interested were asked to become Patrons and to subscribe whatever money they could afford.

When the Royal Court was taken the name of the supporters' group had been changed, first to the Royal Court Theatre Society and then to the English Stage Society.

Through the years membership of the Society has varied greatly. After the initial appeal for patrons, full membership was granted for one guinea, student membership for five shillings, and associate membership – introduced in 1965 for the Club production of *A Patriot for Me* – for seven shillings and sixpence. The associate membership, at first granted for one year and later reduced to three months, allowed the holder all the privileges of the Society except use of the Club. In January 1957, the English Stage Company had granted the Society members priority booking privileges for *The Entertainer* and the membership rolls soared from a few patrons to 906 full members. By the following year, however, about fifty per cent of the membership subscriptions had lapsed. In May 1965, total membership was approximately 1,600. With the announcement that the English Stage Society would produce *A Patriot for Me* – which had been banned from public performance by the Lord Chamberlain (dealt with more fully in Chapter 4) – membership increased to 3,950 in a month and eventually to nearly 10,000. The membership has continued to fluctuate in response to immediate attractions in spite of all attempts to create a loyal body of supporters. But the English Stage Society has contributed greatly to the programme of the English Stage Company.

The most exciting contribution has been its 'Sunday Night Productions Without Decor', which began with Charles Robinson's *The Correspondence Course* on 26 May 1957. The 'Sunday Night' plays were rehearsed up to dress-rehearsal point, but performed with only indications of locale and costumes, as any play is to be seen in the final period before the scenery and costumes arrive. The play cannot be 'dolled up' by production, and hence both its strong points and its weak points are plainly visible. It is an invaluable aid to the budding playwright to be able to see his play in production, even though it may not be considered good enough for a full production. The budget is limited to £300, which allows production of plays of a more experimental nature than the more costly main bill productions. Some plays, such as Arnold Wesker's *The Kitchen*, Gwyn Thomas's *The Keep*, and Michael Rosen's *Backbone*, have later been presented in the main bill; and one, Christopher Hampton's *When Did You Last See My Mother* in 1966, was transferred directly into the West End. The 'Sunday Night' plays have also included presentations of well-known works produced in an experimental way, such as Shakespeare's *Twelfth Night* and Wedekind's *Spring Awakening*, and evenings of poetry, jazz, mime, and ballet and improvisational works.

During the first year of the English Stage Company, all the

productions were directed by either George Devine or Tony
Richardson. But the English theatre was suffering not only from a
lack of worthwhile new plays, but also from a dearth of young directors. Part of the purpose of the Sunday productions was therefore
seen as an opportunity to develop new directors as well as new
playwrights, and the success in that field has been inestimable. The
first Sunday production was directed by Peter Coe; the second
production, Michael Hastings' *Yes – And After*, was directed by
John Dexter; and the third production, Kathleen Sully's *The
Waiting of Lester Abbs*, was directed by Lindsay Anderson – his first
excursion from television and film directing into live theatre. Other
directors who have worked on 'Sunday Night' productions include
William Gaskill, Anthony Page, John Bird, Desmond O'Donovan,
John Blatchely, Ann Jellicoe, Keith Johnstone, Jane Howell, Corin
Redgrave and Peter Gill. In July 1959, partly as a result of the great
fund of directing talent discovered through the Sunday productions,
two forms of artistic direction assistants were established at the
Court: associate directors and assistant directors. The associate
directors were attached to the theatre, but received no contract and
no pay. When they directed a Sunday production they received a fee,
subject to the approval of the Artistic Committee. The first three appointments to this category were made to Lindsay Anderson, John
Dexter and William Gaskill. The second category, assistant directors, received £10 per week each and also received a fee when called
upon to do a production. John Bird and Anthony Page received the
first appointments.

The number of actors who have had opportunities of working in
the Sunday productions is legion, and some, such as Colin Blakely,
have received their first important notice as a result. That the value
of this 'laboratory' for writers, actors, and directors was appreciated
by the artists themselves was demonstrated by the fact that they
were the ones who really subsidized the project. Although rehearsals
usually went on for three weeks, the actors received only two guineas
each for each performance and no rehearsal pay at all. The
playwrights received only five guineas on account of ten per cent of
royalties (based on gross receipts) until 1968, when the payment was
increased to £15 on account of royalties. In return, the author's contract provides that if the English Stage Company does not take up its
option on the play, the author then agrees to give the Society ten per
cent of his earnings on that play in the United Kingdom from the sale
of television, radio, and film rights for a period of two years after the
performance at the Royal Court. That money is then used by the
Society for further productions.

From the time of its first Sunday production in May 1957, the
English Stage Society has produced over seventy-five plays in this
series, including John Arden's first play *The Waters of Babylon*, N.
F. Simpson's *A Resounding Tinkle*, Arnold Wesker's *The Kitchen*,
and Edward Bond's *The Pope's Wedding* and *Early Morning*, in addition to twenty-two other events.

One outgrowth of the 'Sunday Night' productions has been the
Theatre Upstairs, also under the auspices of the English Stage Society, but funded by the English Stage Company. This small studio

theatre, which is dealt with in detail in Chapter 5, provides a steady outlet for experiments in a more intimate atmosphere than the main stage of the Royal Court Theatre, and complements, rather than replaces, the 'Sunday Night' productions.

The English Stage Society has also provided financial assistance to the Company. In 1959, the Society undertook to donate to the Company excess of its cash after retaining £500. The Society raised money from its subscriptions, donations, and from film and theatre premières, and by 1968 its financial contribution to the Company since its inception amounted to £11,500, excluding its indirect contribution of approximately £2,000 per annum in publicity of Company plays to its members, and since 1968 the total has increased considerably.

Another scheme conceived to encourage the habit of going to the Court was aimed at the populace of the Royal Borough of Kensington and Chelsea. Councillor Yeoman, who had been invited to attend the English Stage Company's Council meetings, proposed the scheme in December 1966, by which residents of the Royal Court's local borough would be invited to pay £1 at the box office for a card valid for one year, which would then entitle them to buy seats at half price one hour before curtain, if any were still available. He felt that it would be a gesture which showed that the theatre acknowledged itself as an integral part of the life of the borough. Although it was pointed out that even the residents taking advantage of the scheme would have to buy tickets in advance at full price for the productions which proved highly popular, Joe Hodgkinson, representing the Arts Council, said he was disturbed by such a small theatre having a number of schemes for cheaper seats (the Court also had students' schemes and reduced rates for English Stage Society previews). He also said that the Arts Council were not in favour of local boroughs having special facilities. Nevertheless, the Committee accepted the scheme in the hope that it would serve to increase the regular audience and that it would encourage the Kensington–Chelsea Borough Council to increase its annual grant of 200 guineas. The Company's interest in the scheme, however, diminished and it was never put into operation.

The most ambitious and, ultimately, most far-reaching 'audience development' schemes operated by the English Stage Company have been the various schools schemes. The original brochure of the English Stage Company gave as one of the original aims:

> 'To encourage children to develop a genuine enthusiasm for and critical appreciation of good theatre. To achieve this our repertory ... will include seasons of plays intended for younger theatregoers; these will also be toured wherever educational authorities and schools offer facilities.'

There had been no programme developed by 1960, however, when the Artistic Committee's *Memorandum on Artistic Policy* was produced. But, prompted by that *Memorandum*, the Court was ready to undertake a programme when outside interest was shown.

The immediate impetus for the initial project was a letter received from two English teachers in Hertfordshire. They occasionally brought parties to the Royal Court and other theatres and said that it was very sad that while within their school there were all kinds of extra-mural activities in the sciences, there was never any field work in the arts. George Devine sent his assistant, John Blatchley, to meet with the two teachers and he worked out a plan for group visits.

The first group of sixteen students, between the ages of sixteen and eighteen, came from Hertfordshire for a week's visit in the autumn of 1960 and after press publicity and word-of-mouth, more groups began arriving. Because of the amount of time and effort involved the Company could cope with only one group a month.

The group would arrive on a Monday morning and would stay through until the following Friday evening or Saturday morning. Blatchley or one of the other assistants would meet them at the Court and they would first be taken around the theatre and told a bit about the English Stage Company, what it stood for, and what it was doing. During their stay, the group would go to some theatre at least once a day and sometimes twice – matinée and evening. They would see rehearsals at the Royal Court and rehearsals in another theatre; they would watch students training at the Central School of Speech Training and Dramatic Art; they would tour some kind of workshop: wardrobe or carpenter or paint or prop; they would visit a designer, preferably one whose work they had seen during the week. The lighting man at the Court would take a whole morning to talk about lighting and to show them lighting. The stage director would take them all over the theatre and show them the flies, the grids, the lifts. The front of the house manager would talk to them and the box office manager would talk to them. The assistant directors would take them to the various theatres.

The fare of the plays varied. Sometimes the group would be taken to a play which the people from the Court thought was fairly ridiculous, such as Agatha Christie's *The Mousetrap*. Sometimes they would go to an opera or a ballet; sometimes they would go to popular things, sometimes they would go to classical things. Sometimes George Devine would take them to a boxing or wrestling match. The aim was to give them a taste of the whole range of theatre. At the end of the week they would have a session with one person whose work they had seen on stage who could be persuaded to meet them: it might be Vanessa Redgrave or Peter Bull, or any actor, director, or designer. That person would have an open discussion with them about what they had felt about their experiences.

The charge for the whole week of theatre was £1, which covered fares within the city and the cost of all tickets. Other theatres cooperated by giving reduced prices, or free seats if the play were not doing very well. But the students had to provide their own food and they had to live within daily travelling distance of the Royal Court or stay with relatives who did.

In the autumn of 1961 George Devine was ill and had to take time away from the theatre. Tony Richardson temporarily took over as Artistic Director and wanted to expand the schools programme even further. John Blatchley again devised a programme, much more grandiose than the visits scheme. However, although Neville Blond offered to give £1,000 to help initiate the project, various problems, especially those of space and personnel, arose and the Schools Scheme was discontinued until 1966. This is dealt with in some detail in Chapter 5.

The objective of forming links with provincial repertory theatres was a natural outgrowth of the original aims of the Company. One objective announced at the Kingsway Theatre had been 'to play at those towns which do not maintain live theatre but could support an occasional visit from a first-class company'. That objective had been well-served from the beginning. *Look Back in Anger* had been played at a number of the larger provincial cities during the spring and summer of 1957 and had had an extensive Arts Council tour of smaller cities in the autumn and winter of 1957. *The Country Wife* had played at Oxford and Brighton before opening at the Royal Court, and *Requiem for a Nun* had opened at Bournemouth for a week's run and moved to Blackpool for a week before arriving at the Court. The practice of presenting Royal Court productions in provincial cities before (and sometimes after) playing at the Royal Court Theatre has remained an important implementation of policy. But it was not the only attempt to encourage theatre in the provinces before 1960.

In July 1957, Neville Blond said that he was anxious for the Company to hold a festival the following summer to give repertory companies in the provinces the opportunity of presenting their work to London audiences. He felt that it would encourage the repertory companies and would provide a chance for directors, designers, actors and actresses to show their worth in the capital. The suggestion was accepted by both the Management and the Artistic Committees. It was decided, in accordance with the Company's basic policy, to select four companies that were prepared to give the first professional production of a new play of contemporary interest, with preference given to a play by an English playwright. Each selected play was offered a run of one week, and all production costs were borne by the English Stage Company.

The four companies which participated were the Citizens Theatre, Glasgow, which presented *Gay Landscape* by George Munro; Belgrade Theatre, Coventry, with *Chicken Soup With Barley* by Arnold Wesker; Salisbury Arts Theatre, with *The Private Prosecutor* by Thomas Wiseman; and the Leatherhead Repertory Theatre, with *Dear Augustine* by Alison Macleod. Although *Gay Landscape* was a genuinely regional piece and *Chicken Soup With Barley* certainly an exceptional 'social' drama, the season was not considered a success either artistically or financially. It seemed that all the new authors sent their scripts directly to the Royal Court. The outstanding artistic success (there was no outstanding financial success) was *Chicken Soup With Barley*[1] and that was directed by John Dexter, an assistant at the Court. The season was a financial disaster: *Gay Landscape* played to only twelve per cent of box office capacity, *Chicken Soup With Barley* to twenty-six per cent, *The Private Prosecutor* to thirty-one per cent, and *Dear Augustine* to nineteen per cent. Although it had been hoped to make the festival an annual event at the Court, the results of the first year discouraged the idea.

The objective proposed by the Artistic Committee in 1960, however, was to form a permanent liaison with from one to three provincial repertory companies. The only implementation of that proposal was the Cambridge Arts Scheme.

During the summer and autumn of 1960 negotiations were being carried out with a number of repertory companies. William Gaskill had been conducting a series of readings of new plays at Cambridge in order to help new playwrights who had not yet been produced at the Royal Court and the most satisfactory scheme evolved from discussions between Gaskill and Stanley Pye, of Pye Radio, who was very anxious to revitalize the Arts Theatre in Cambridge. The scheme was set out in January 1961, and it was noted that it was within the framework of the *Memorandum on Artistic Policy*.

The scheme was seen to be the first of a series of such link-ups with the provinces. The English Stage Company sought the association because it was badly in need of a studio or auxiliary theatre to develop the talent it had discovered over the preceding five years, which it was incapable of developing itself either because of economic pressures or because the programme was too full. The 'Sunday Night' productions were not completely satisfactory because the rehearsal time was limited and it was becoming increasingly difficult to persuade actors to appear for the token payment of two guineas.

The Cambridge Arts Theatre, although of a great reputation in the past, had no consistent policy and no resident company. It was virtually a touring theatre with occasional productions under its own management and certain commitments to university and amateur groups. Built by John Maynard Keynes at his own expense in 1936 and presented in trust to the city and university in 1938, the theatre was administered through a committee under the chairmanship of George Rylands. Because of the Trust, it was perhaps the only provincial theatre capable of developing a non-commercial policy.

The basic idea of the scheme was to form a company of actors at the Arts Theatre with a policy based on that of the Royal Court – the development of new writers – run by an Artistic Director (Gaskill) and involving an exchange of productions between the two theatres. The company would operate for a thirty-six week period from October to June, covering the period of the three university terms. Since the town was not large enough to support shows for more than one week, and as it would be impossible to maintain a good standard of production on less than three weeks' rehearsal, the company would have to play one week at Cambridge and two weeks elsewhere.

The programme would consist of ten productions – five revivals or classics and five new plays. The five new plays would largely take over the function of the 'Sunday Night' productions, and also some of the more doubtful of the main bill productions. It was suggested that the five new plays should either play at the Court for one week each following their opening week at Cambridge or that the new plays be presented at the Court for a short repertory season at the end of the Cambridge season. Whenever possible, the Royal Court productions would be tried out in Cambridge prior to opening in London. The Cambridge stage was large enough to take most Court productions and had provision for a fore-stage which could be made into a replica of the one at the Court.

It was calculated that by playing to twenty-five per cent of the financial capacity of £5,000 per week and with a get-out of £1,500, the loss for the new plays would amount to £1,000 per week, or £5,000 for the five shows. That would be no more than the loss on one unsuccessful production in the Court's main bill – i.e. *Murderer's Rock*, or *The Happy Haven,* or *Trials by Logue.*

The advantages to the Cambridge Arts Theatre, then, would be the revitalization of their theatre under the experienced direction of the English Stage Company and the drawing of new plays and artists on their reputation.

The advantages to the English Stage Company would be an easing of the burden of incessant production of new works, the opportunity of five new plays being presented under better conditions than was possible with Sunday shows, a saving on plays of doubtful financial success, the advantage of a permanent tryout theatre, and a regular outlet for unused talent.

The Calouste Gulbenkian Foundation made a grant of £3,000 to enable the Arts Theatre and the English Stage Company to launch the scheme and on 6 October 1961, Edward Albee's *The American Dream* and *The Death of Bessie Smith* opened at the Cambridge Arts Theatre prior to a three weeks' run at the Court. During the short duration of the liaison, two new plays were produced at the Cambridge Arts: Ann Jellicoe's *The Knack*, which opened at Cambridge on 13 October 1961, and played for a week there before moving to Bath and Cardiff for a week in each; and Henry Chapman's *That's Us,* which opened for a week's run on 30 October before going to the Royal Court for a week, followed by a week in Exeter. One revival, *Arden of Faversham*, was produced and opened at Cambridge on 20 November, before moving to Cardiff and Exeter. Then the money ran out.

The experiment, though short-lived, could hardly be called a total disaster. *The Knack*, which the Royal Court wasn't going to produce, was a success and went on to the Royal Court, the West End, and the films. And Nicol Williamson was discovered as an actor. It was found to be much harder to start a new experimental play in the provinces than in London, but if the project had become financially viable, it would have been continued.

The immediate proposal for fulfilling the objective of a larger theatre was to accept part in a joint venture with Laurence Olivier Productions and Oscar Lewenstein Productions at the Metropolitan Theatre, Edgware Road, London. The Metropolitan, an old music hall which had been turned into a television studio, was available in 1960 and it was hoped that the joint venture would allow experiment by all three of the partners. The basic advantages it offered the English Stage Company would be the ability to develop a more popular audience – the 1,500-seat Metropolitan would allow a higher percentage of cheap seats – and the space needed for the larger shows. It would also allow the Company to exploit its successes more fully. However, after a great deal of work by all three parties, the project fell through. The Metropolitan, it was learned, was in the path of a new highway project and was therefore in danger of demolition; and, shortly after, the National Theatre at last came into being, thus drawing Olivier out of the group.[2]

Instead of finding a new theatre, it was decided to improve the Royal Court. It is worth studying the rebuilding schemes proposed for the Royal Court for three reasons: (1) the recognition of the limitations inherent in the Royal Court Theatre; (2) the proposed solution to those problems; (3) the reasons those proposed solutions were not carried out.

The Royal Court had been a small theatre seating 439 in three tiers: stalls, dress circle, and upper circle. The proscenium stage was altered slightly by the addition of a forestage when the English Stage Company took over the theatre, but it still remained basically an inflexible proscenium stage with very little space in the wings. As such, the amount of experimentation possible in production methods was severely limited. In January 1963, when the Company was considering reconstruction of the theatre, George Devine said that he would like any reconstruction scheme to be considered in conjunction with an entirely new image for the theatre artistically. He hoped to be able to present plays in a new style which, he believed, would in turn attract new writing.

The original plan was to completely demolish and reconstruct the building, to include bars, restaurant, and, possibly, a studio theatre. The cost was estimated at £100,000, but the new seating capacity would create an increased financial capacity of £18,698 per year at one hundred per cent capacity, or £9,349 per year at the normally budgeted fifty per cent of capacity. As a long-term investment, then, the plan was feasible.

But the English Stage Company's lease on the Royal Court had only twenty-eight years to run. Alfred Esdaile said that provided the Company could obtain a new lease, he considered the reconstruction plans to be sound; but, failing that, he would advise against spending more than £20,000–£30,000. Esdaile also warned that estimates are often lower than the actual cost of a project.

Greville Poke and Alfred Esdaile approached Lord Cadogan of Cadogan Estates, the landlord of the Royal Court, with the Company's plans. Lord Cadogan appreciated the Company's desire to improve the building and was conscious of the importance of its work and expressed a desire to help in every way possible. But he felt it was unwise for the Company to go in for any large capital expenditure with the lease as short as it was, and, in view of development plans for Sloane Square, which were not yet settled, he could not see his way to an extension of the lease. He said that the whole area, including the Royal Court Theatre, was under consideration and might become a major development scheme in conjunction with the Grosvenor Estate. However, whatever development took place, there would always be a theatre because the London County Council insisted upon it.

By November 1963, it became apparent that the original estimates probably would be only half the actual cost. Joe Hodgkinson, representing the Arts Council, said that the Company could not possibly continue operating in the theatre in its existing condition, but also thought it undesirable for the theatre to remain closed for too long. Devine had devised a second, less inclusive, scheme which could be effected if the total reconstruction could not be realized. This scheme involved mainly, re-decoration, new bars, and improvements to such things as lighting, plumbing, and storage. The second plan would not involve any basic structural changes and would not improve the structure of the stage – hence, Devine's hopes to have a stage which would allow for more experimental production methods would be dashed.

Lord Cadogan offered an extension of the lease, but with the condition that he could exercise a breach at the end of the existing lease if he so chose. Although it was the best he could offer under the circumstances of his own uncertain re-development plans, it would not provide a trustee security, which was needed in order to raise the money required for the major reconstruction. On 18 December 1963, after a year of planning, the Management Committee reluctantly decided that the Company could not proceed with the major reconstruction scheme. Instead, the modified scheme of improvements, with a limit of £20,000, was effected and an additional £2,500 spent on maintenance. The limited programme of improvement was basically financed by a gift of £5,000 from Neville Blond, an Arts Council capital grant of £15,000 (representing three years' grants), and surplus funds which had been built up. But the budget for certain items was exceeded. Jocelyn Herbert and George Devine paid for the difference for lighting fixtures between the actual cost and the budgeted cost (Atlas Lighting Company had already given a discount of fifty per cent); Greville Poke and Robin Fox paid for large mirrors, which had not been included in the budget; Alfred Esdaile paid for carpeting.

During the rebuilding, from March until September 1964, the English Stage Company did indeed move to a larger theatre – The Queen's in London's West End, in which the Company was associated with H. M. Tennent Productions and Lewenstein-Delfont Productions. George Devine remained Artistic Director of the Company, while Anthony Page became Artistic Director at the Royal Court and worked out the season to take place after the theatre's reopening.

Three plays were planned for the West End season, with Vanessa Redgrave to appear in each. *The Seagull*, with Peggy Ashcroft playing Madame Arkadina, Vanessa Redgrave as Nina, George Devine as Dorn, Paul Rogers as Sorin, Peter McEnery as Konstantin, Peter Finch as Trigorin, Rachel Kempson as Polina, and Ann Beach as Masha, opened on 4 March 1964, and had a very successful run until its scheduled closing on 30 May. Brecht's *St Joan of the Stockyards* followed on 8 June. Vanessa Redgrave became ill, but, fortunately, another star, Siobhan McKenna, was able to step in. But even with her great talent, the play was not successful. The third play was to have been *The World's Baby* by Michael Hastings, but it was decided that the script was not up to standard and couldn't be produced without rewriting. Although replacements were considered, Vanessa Redgrave's continued illness forced the season to close on 27 June. The West End Season thus only partly fulfilled two of its basic purposes: to keep the name of the English Stage Company before the public; and to provide an outlet for talent. Thus, there were no productions for over two months until 9 September, when the Royal Court reopened with John Osborne's new play, *Inadmissible Evidence*, starring Nicol Williamson.

The idea of training for actors was inherent in George Devine's total philosophy of theatre practice. He believed that training should not stop as soon as an actor got his first job. He tried to implement his ideas the first year by having the permanent company go through a series of exercises before each day's rehearsals. But with an already heavy rehearsal and performance schedule, the actors did not take kindly to the added joys of strenuous exercises early in the morning, and eventually the project was dropped. After the dissolution of the permanent company the exercises proved even more unworkable, but Devine and his assistants continued to feel that a studio was needed.

In the autumn of 1962 the Company learned that the Jeannetta Cochrane Theatre, which had not yet been opened to the public, was available and could be had for free. The Jeannetta Cochrane was built by the Central School of Arts and Crafts, of which Jocelyn Herbert, a frequent designer at the Court, was a trustee. William Gaskill had been teaching quite a lot for the British Drama League and had also taught his own course at the City Literary Institute, one of the Greater London Council's marvellous institutes which are open to anyone at very little cost. Gaskill had taught two terms there, working in techniques connected with comic performing. A lot of the work he did was with comic masks – the half, or character, mask – which Gaskill had learned from George Devine, who had used the technique while teaching at the Old Vic Theatre School. During that series of classes Gaskill met Claude Chagrin, who attended as a student but who had also been extremely well-trained in mime by Jacques Lecoq in Paris. At the Central School of Speech Training and Dramatic Art, Gaskill had also done comic improvisational work which was loosely called 'clowning' – comic improvisation often of a slapstick nature. This background of experience was brought to and largely influenced the shape of the English Stage Company Theatre studio, which was organized under the direction of Gaskill.

In January 1963, the Management Committee voted £50 to get the project started and it was immediately publicized. The first term the students were charged only two shillings and sixpence for the whole course, with no restriction on entry whatsoever. George Devine, Claude Chagrin, Keith Johnstone, and Gaskill taught a term which was loosely called 'comedy'. Devine taught what he called 'comic tricks', or 'the comedian's tricks', which were all the things like double-takes and pratfalls, and the whole repertoire of the physical comic techniques. Chagrin taught mime. Gaskill taught various things: comic improvisation, the comic mask, and a class which he called 'the epic narrative', which was based on the Brechtian method concerned with narrative analysis. Johnstone also had a class which was concerned with the narrative and the fairy tale. On 28 April 1963, the Studio presented a 'Sunday Night' show called *First Results* in which each class demonstrated the work done that first term.

In April the Company voted another £20 to keep the project going. Gaskill, who had moved to the National Theatre with John Dexter and Laurence Olivier, still was not being paid extra for the teaching – nor were any of the Court personnel. But, with the success of the first term behind them, the Company applied to the Calouste Gulbenkian Trust for a grant to enable them to continue the Studio on a more permanent basis. The Gulbenkian responded with £2,500 per year for three years. It had also been decided that the Studio would be run in conjunction with the National Theatre and they made a payment towards the expense. But, in practice, it didn't work out. It proved impossible to fit in times of attendance at the Studio by actors working in a permanent repertory company. Nevertheless, the English Stage Company Theatre Studio was the only professional acting studio – as distinct from the drama schools for training entrants to the profession – connected with the acting profession as a whole, not being confined to one particular company.

In September 1963, the Studio, still at the Jeannetta Cochrane, opened under Keith Johnstone's direction, though Gaskill continued to teach when time permitted. Johnstone developed the work that the earlier Studio had set out to do – the comic work and the improvisational work. In 1965, Johnstone presented a Christmas show, *Clowning*, in the main bill of the Royal Court, which was totally developed from the work of the Studio. *Clowning* was an improvised show: there was no written script of any kind – though there was an extremely loose structure – and all the actors changed parts for different performances. The group which performed *Clowning* has remained intact and – as the Theatre Machine – has worked consistently since then.

The improvisational work which led to and made up *Clowning* ante-dated the other apparently related *avant-garde* movements in the fringe theatre, such as the Living Theatre; but *Clowning* is very different in kind: although certainly related to the *Commedia dell'Arte*, its more immediate inspiration is the English music hall tradition. Indeed, the use of improvisation is the only point of contact with the Living Theatre, for *Clowning* and the Theatre Machine are essentially concerned with making people laugh.

The Theatre Studio continued operations into 1965, when Gaskill became Artistic Director of the English Stage Company. By then it had expanded beyond its original boundaries and visited Youth Centres in the provinces where it gave short courses in experimental techniques. These visits not only advanced the influence of the Studio, but also provided a source of income necessary to the Studio's continued operation. By the summer of 1965, with the National Theatre's financial support withdrawn, that additional income was very important. In August, with the expense of the new permanent acting company and the risk of reverting to repertory coming up, N. V. Linklater of the Arts Council suggested that the Arts Council, while acknowledging the importance of the work of the Theatre Studio, might consider that it was something which could be excluded from the budget. Gaskill, however, felt that the value of the Studio was incalculable for the little money spent, and determined to continue it. But, although the Management Committee approved continued support for the Studio and the Gulbenkian grant was still in effect, it lasted only one more term, the autumn of 1965. The English Stage Company was forced to end the scheme for much the same reason that the National Theatre had earlier withdrawn: it became impossible to operate in conjunction with a permanent acting company performing in repertory.

This reversion to the permanent repertory company, which will be dealt with in detail in Chapter 5, was initiated by Gaskill when he accepted the position of Artistic Director of the English Stage Company in January 1965.

George Devine had been suffering from exhaustion and ill health for some time before he made the decision to relinquish his position as Artistic Director. For ten years he had guided the Company through its constant crises and had literally worn himself out. Even if his health had not failed, Devine would have retired as active Artistic Director. He felt that he had carried the Company as far as he could, that new blood was needed if the Company were going to remain vital and alive. On 25 January 1965, at the annual Critics' Luncheon given by Neville Blond at the Savoy Hotel, George Devine announced his resignation as Artistic Director of the English Stage Company. After summing up the accomplishments of his nine years with the Company – 145 productions and 87 'Sunday Nights', of which 126 were plays by contemporary English writers more or less discovered by the Royal Court, twenty assistant directors 'to suck one's blood and pass on to be vampired elsewhere' – he explained why he was leaving:

> 'Perhaps I could recollect in paraphrase a remark of Gide's: when a man begins to feel he is part of the fixtures and fittings, it is time he left. I am deeply tired. The weight of this edifice has driven me into the ground up to my neck, like poor Winnie in *Happy Days*. I should have passed the job on several years ago. I thought I should see it through. I damned nearly did. I am getting out just in time.'

He then went on to give advice to Gaskill:

> 'As I pass on to fresh fields and pastures new – if unknown to me as yet – I can promise my successor adventurous flying: plenty of bumps; many anxious glances at the petrol gauge, most of the time in thick, stormy cloud; occasional, very occasional, glimpses of the nearest thing to paradise. And my only advice to him is: keep your best eye on your horizon, the other on your instruments, and, for God's sake, fasten your seat belts before you take off.'

Devine had not founded the English Stage Company, but he had provided its soul. He created an atmosphere where people could fail – where they could try, and learn, and fail, and grow. At the beginning he was directing plays, acting very often, and directing the theatre, all with very little money. But this greatness lay in his desire and ability to encourage talent, to help other people to be as good as they could be. He wasn't a great actor, but he was a good actor and an unselfish actor – he always acted *with* people. When his assistants were directing he always knew what was going on in the productions. His office was just off the upper circle and he would slip in unbeknown to the director and actors. If the director later came to him with a problem, he was able to help him. He taught without seeming to teach. A mixture of austerity and good-humoured gentleness, George Devine created a theatre where people loved to work, a theatre free from the pettiness and 'camp' which are so common in other theatres. Although he had had a distinguished career before joining the English Stage Company, his work and achievements at the Royal Court are his testimonial and his affirmation.

The Artistic Committee, faced with the task of finding a replacement for Devine, considered three possibilities: (1) to realize the assets of the Company and to wind it up; (2) to let the theatre; (3) to continue the existing policy if a suitable successor to Devine could be found.

The first suggestion was immediately ruled out by the Artistic Committee.

The Committee had then considered the possibility of a liaison with the National Theatre and/or the Royal Shakespeare Company whereby they might be able to take over the Royal Court for their own productions for long periods. Preliminary sounding with both companies had shown that they were interested in this suggestion.

However, it was the wish of the Artistic Committee that the Company should continue its existing policy provided that a suitable Artistic Director could be found, and, when the announcement of Devine's retirement had been made, a number of applications for the position had been received including one from William Gaskill. Besides his past association with the English Stage Company, Gaskill had developed an independent reputation as a director and was an experienced Artistic Director with the National Theatre. He was anxious to continue the policy of the Company and was willing to serve for a minimum of three years. With his outstanding qualifications as recommendation, it was decided, over the objection of Ronald Duncan, to appoint Gaskill Artistic Director of the English Stage Company. He took over the position in July 1965, when his contract with the National Theatre expired.

Devine, when he submitted his resignation, had agreed to retain his position until the following September. He was to act in one more show before his retirement – John Osborne's *A Patriot for Me*, which had been banned by the Lord Chamberlain. Although he was much too tired to do it, he played the role of Baron Von Epp, the drag queen of the tranvestite ball. He took the role because none of the agents would let their actors play homosexuals. When Devine said he would play the queen, the agents felt much better about it and it was possible to complete the casting. And Devine gave one of the best performances of his career.

Unfortunately, he was unable to pass on to fresh fields. On 22 January 1966, after a series of heart attacks, George Devine died. Among the many obituaries, the *Sunday Times* briefly and eloquently paid tribute to one of the greatest men in modern theatre history:

'George Devine was one of the three important animating figures

of the post-war theatre. He was the complement of Peter Hall and
Laurence Olivier. They have made a producer's theatre and an actor's theatre. At the Royal Court, Devine made a writer's theatre,
stamping it with his own thought and independent personality . . .
Devine made the English Stage Company the principal socially
conscious theatre in the English-speaking world.

'Devine had success both as an actor and as a director; but it is
as the father-figure of the Royal Court that he accomplished work
as valuable as any that has been done in contemporary theatre. He
will, as his bold and active temperament would have wished, be
criticized (there are theatrical managers who consider the English
Stage Company to be the greatest misfortune that ever happened
to the British drama); but he will not be forgotten.'

George Devine's work was already being carried on by his student
and friend, William Gaskill. Gaskill had returned to the original
policy of producing plays in repertory using a permanent company of
actors, and he was championing a new playwright, Edward Bond,
even though the Lord Chamberlain had banned his play, *Saved*.
However, whereas at the outset Devine had received an Arts Council
grant of only £5,000 and was caught from the first in the balancing
act of having financial success pay for financial failure, the Arts
Council grant to the English Stage Company had risen to £50,425 by
1965–6. It was not any sudden flash of enlightenment that caused the
Arts Council to increase their grants: the Arts Council, although
providing limited financial support, had been involved in the success
of the Company from the beginning.

Although the Arts Council distributes its money in many ways, the
Royal Court has received its support mainly through three types of
grants: direct subsidy, guarantees against loss, and capital expenditure grants. The direct subsidy is agreed upon through negotiations between the Company and the Arts Council and the amount is
determined by three main factors: the proven need, the Arts Council's judgement of the value of the work being done, and the amount
of funds available to the Arts Council. There is great leeway for
negotiations within this framework of reference, but the main
deterrent to increased subsidy has usually been the Arts Council's
lack of financial resources. The guarantee against loss is a method
whereby the Arts Council earmarks money, beyond the outright subsidy, which can be drawn upon if the subsidy does not cover the
theatre's deficit during a given financial year. But the guarantee
against loss is not cumulative and cannot be put in a reserve fund for
future needs, as can the subsidy. The capital expenditure grants,
which have been totally inadequate at best, are made separately from
the subsidy for the purpose of maintenance and improvements to the
real property of the theatre.

The subsidy, the principal grant the English Stage Company
receives from the Arts Council, is granted on a yearly basis, not for an
individual play. Although the Arts Council is concerned with the
Company's policy and the general implementation of that policy, it is
not its business to pass judgement on any individual play. That is an
extremely important point of Arts Council policy. Lord Keynes

stressed that very point in 1945 when he said:

> 'Everyone, I fancy, recognizes that the work of the artists in all its
> aspects is, of its nature, individual and free, undisciplined, un-
> regimented, uncontrolled. The artist walks where the breath of
> the spirit blows him. He cannot be told of his direction; he does
> not know it himself. But he leads the rest of us into fresh pastures
> and teaches us to love and to enjoy what we often begin by rejec-
> ting, enlarging our sensibility and purifying our instincts. *The
> task of an official body is not to teach or to censor, but to give
> courage, confidence, and opportunity* [my italics].'³

The initial offer of £500 had been raised to £2,500 pre-production
with a further £5,000 grant for the first year's operations when
Neville Blond announced that he was backing the Company as chairman. There seem to be two main reasons for this great increase.
First, Neville Blond offered business experience and stability. The
Arts Council in those days was much more conservative than it is
today: it didn't have very much money and it was much more concerned with formal questions – such as the system of accounting, the
'respectability' of the board. The second reason is that the English
Stage Company before Neville Blond came in was not permanently
based and didn't seem likely to become what it in fact did. Even the
founders were amazed to find themselves with a theatre. Then, too, the
Arts Council is not really an innovative body. It has always been its
policy to support local and private initiative, not to initiate projects
itself. When considering the very small sum of the £5,000 grant, it
should also be noted that in the same year, 1955–6, the Old Vic was
receiving only £15,000 and the most highly subsidized provincial
repertory theatre in the country, Nottingham, was receiving only
£3,000.

The 'local initiative' was purely private in the case of the English
Stage Company. The Royal Borough of Chelsea (the Royal Boroughs
of Kensington and Chelsea were amalgamated on 1 April 1965)
provided no support and has never provided more than the most
paltry support. Although empowered to levy a six-old-pence rate in
support of the arts (a one-tenth-of-one-penny rate would yield approximately £10,000 annually), the Royal Court's local borough has
provided grants of only £100 to £200 per year. In fact, in January,
1965, a Councillor moved to withhold the grant altogether because he
had read about the farewell luncheon at the Savoy for George
Devine. He questioned how they could give lunches at the Savoy if
the Company had such a serious cash deficit. No one seconded the
motion and the grant of 200 guineas was made. The luncheon, which
was a combination of the farewell dinner and the annual Critics'
Luncheon, was, as always, paid for by Neville Blond.

Another, more important, source of financial support has been the
London County Council, later the Greater London Council. In 1958
the L.C.C. was beginning to get involved with financing the arts,
stemming from their big project in building and operating the
Festival Hall which they had built on the South Bank in 1951.
Although the L.C.C. did not feel itself to be in a position to help until

1961, it then granted £2,500 to the English Stage Company, a figure which it has held to each year since.

Industry has provided another source of income through the years. When George Devine and Tony Richardson had tried to start their theatre for writers prior to the founding of the English Stage Company, they had approached O. B. Miller, Chairman and Managing Director of the John Lewis Partnership (the large department store company), in hopes that he would agree to support them (the Partnership already helped to support the Glyndebourne Touring Opera). Miller offered them some support, but not enough by itself to start the project. However, Devine mentioned the earlier contact to the Company and Miller was asked to join the Council in 1956. He brought with him £2,000 as a loan (though no one ever expected to see their 'loans' paid back in those days) and he also was prepared to allow the Company to buy materials at cost price at one of his department stores, Peter Jones, just across Sloane Square from the Royal Court. Another supporter from industry was the late Sir Frederic Hooper, Chairman and Managing Director of Schweppes, Ltd, who joined the Council of the Company in 1958. Through Sir Frederic, Schweppes underwrote the production of Ann Jellicoe's *The Sport of My Mad Mother* in 1958, up to £1,000. Sir Frederic also encouraged other support from industry through the years. One of the more surprising industry grants came from Oxo, Ltd – surprising not because of its size, but because it was made at all. At a ceremony at the Royal Court on 11 September 1958, T. A. H. Sycamore, Managing Director of Oxo, presented the English Stage Company with a check for £1,000 on behalf of his firm. He made the gift 'on a note of slight criticism of policy and what is being done, and regretted the failure to discover a new Shakespeare whose work was devoid of sex, blasphemy, anti-monarchical opinions, and sensational things which don't make true theatre.'[4]

Nevertheless, however important the other grants and discounts have been, it is the Arts Council to whom the Company inevitably turned for its largest continuing support. But it would be wrong, too, to believe that the English Stage Company either began operations or remained in operation primarily because of Arts Council support. From April 1956, until April 1965 – when the Arts Council grant increased dramatically – the Company had earned £169,823, an average of £18,869 per year, from transfers, tours, and the sale of film and production rights. These figures compare with total Arts Council grants of £113,500 for the period, or an average of £12,611 per year – a figure in itself deceptive since for the first six years the average was only £6,416 per year. But when the Company was in serious financial difficulties – and it often was – the Arts Council helped as much as it could within the bounds of its limited resources.

The financial year ending 31 March 1958 had showed a large surplus for the Company, but by October that surplus had been depleted at an alarming rate. O. B. Miller pointed out that the Artistic Committee had chosen plays which they considered worthy of presentation, but the Committee obviously could not guarantee their success, and that if the Company continued to lose money at such a rapid rate as it had been doing, the reserves would soon be exhausted and the

Company would have no alternative but to close. It was essential to obtain some form of permanent financial assistance if the Company were to continue to function. He said that the Arts Council should be approached, shown what the Company had achieved in the past, and presented with the current accounts together with a programme for the future so they could see for themselves the inadequacy of their grants. He estimated that, operating at the current rate of loss, an annual grant of £25,000 would be needed. It was finally agreed to apply for a grant of £20,000 for 1959–60. By April 1959, the immediate danger of collapse had been averted and the Arts Council responded with a grant of only £5,000, but assured the Company that they could depend on the Arts Council for help if and when needed. By November it was estimated that the deficit would reach £31,000 by the end of the year. The Council of the English Stage Company realized that the Arts Council could not contribute anything like that amount, and agreed that unless some other source of financial support were found, it was inevitable that the theatre would have to close.

One answer to the financial crisis had already been tried: the production of Noel Coward's Feydeaul adaptation, *Look After Lulu*, with Vivien Leigh playing the lead. The play was quite frankly chosen to make money, to allow the theatre to survive. The play proved a financial success, but George Devine and Tony Richardson knew what they had done: they had used something they didn't believe in in order to survive; they had supported the kind of mindless farce that the English Stage Company opposed so much. The Company had desperately needed money and Tony Richardson had said, 'All right, I'll do the fucking thing'; but it was bad because they didn't believe in it and if keeping the theatre open meant presenting more of that sort of play, it would be admitting the greatest defeat of purpose in order to survive – and simple survival is not what good theatre is about.

Improved box office receipts, overdrafts guaranteed by Neville Blond, and the sale of rights again pulled the Company through the crisis. But the income and expenditure results continued to follow the same pattern: there was a big deficit on the Company's activities and that deficit was partly met by income from outside sources, including the Arts Council grant. It was obvious that the Company was dependent on those external financial sources for their survival, but it was income derived from the sale of film and production rights and from transfers which kept pulling the Company out of difficulties. It was also obvious that the Company could not plan on the basis of that uncertain income.

In 1961 the Company again found itself in danger of financial collapse. The Arts Council was approached for a supplementary grant, but had not funds available. However, the Arts Council did assure the Company that their support for the financial year 1962–3 would be increased to £20,000, including a guarantee against loss – a 150 per cent increase over the previous year.

Nevertheless, the financial fortunes of the English Stage Company continued to be precarious and the Company records show that Neville Blond guaranteed overdrafts in January 1963 and again in

May 1963, and that the Arts Council gave an advance on the regular grant in March 1963.

One benefit was finally gained in July 1964 when, after years of consideration, the Royal Borough of Chelsea granted a fifty per cent reduction in rates because the English Stage Company was a registered charity. Although other local authorities had long granted tax relief to theatres registered as charities, the Chelsea Council had balked because admission was charged, as it is in every theatre which is registered as a non-profit-distributing charity. In 1964 that concession represented a saving for the Company of approximately £1,000. In real terms, at today's rates it means that the English Stage Company pays the Royal Borough of Kensington and Chelsea approximately £1,900 a year – and received a grant of only £150.

In August 1964, George Devine had prepared a short paper which showed that because of rising costs, any amount of planning made it impossible to produce a play then as economically as in 1956. He concluded that if the Company were to continue to present new plays it must be prepared for substantial losses and could continue with the policy of new plays only if the grants were sufficient to cover those losses. It was further pointed out that as there were no new plays of merit available, the Company was forced to do revivals and classics (*Waiting for Godot* and *Julius Caesar* were both scheduled for the autumn). The Company was limited in its ability to take risks by the small financial assistance in the form of grants and if more money would be forthcoming it would be easier to take the financial risks and to present new plays of an experimental nature. In the past those plays had averaged a loss of £5,000 per production. Neville Blond pointed out that in eight years the Company had produced approximately 150 new plays and that he would like to continue doing so. In fact, (he pointed out with a combination of wit and business acumen), there was the new Ben Travers farce, *Cuckoo in the Nest*, which he thought might provide food for thought for new writers.[5]

In October 1964, George Devine presented detailed budgets through the year ending 31 March 1966 – submitted on the assumption that it was desired to keep the Company on an established basis as England's only real experimental theatre, whose work would subsequently fertilize the theatre at large. Whereas the Company had previously worked with an inadequate establishment, he considered that the Company should aim to achieve a reasonable establishment with salaries comparable to other institutional theatres so as to achieve maximum efficiency, and that establishment and those salaries were incorporated in the estimates. He also suggested that estimates for the next five years could be made, adding a five per cent increase to all items annually, which would conform to the experience of rising costs over the previous nine years.

Thus, with constantly increasing costs and steady optimism, the Company entered 1965 with an interest-free loan of £7,500 from the Arts Council.[6]

The Arts Council grant (including guarantees against loss) had risen from the original level of £5,000 to £32,500 by the 1964–5 financial year. While that rise was considerable, it must be placed against the rise of the Treasury grants-in-aid to the Arts Council: £820,000 in 1955–6 to £3,205,000 in the 1964–5 financial year. During that same time the Arts Council grant to the Royal Opera House, Covent Garden, had risen from £250,000 to £1,055,000. While no one would suggest that the English Stage Company should have received or needed a subsidy anywhere near that of the Covent Garden, the disproportion certainly raises questions of the appropriateness of such financial stringency by the Arts Council when making grants to a company of such obvious and proven value to the English theatre as the English Stage Company. Nevertheless, although the 1965–6 grant of £50,425 did not guarantee absolute financial security, it did provide Gaskill with a new freedom.

### Notes

1. *Chicken Soup with Barley* was revived at the Royal Court on 7 January 1960.
2. The Metropolitan Theatre was demolished in 1964.
3. Lord Keynes, 'The Arts Council: Its Policy and Hopes,' *Listener*, 12 July 1945, p. 1.
4. 'Company Grant,' *The Times*, 12 September 1958.
5. *Cuckoo in the Nest* was presented at the Royal Court Theatre on 22 October 1964, and lost money.
6. The loan was subsequently converted into a supplementary grant.

# 4 Censorship

'*DIE MARTIS*, 17° Maii, 1966 Censorship of the Theatre —
MOVED, that it is desirable that a Joint Committee of both
Houses be appointed to review the law and practice relating to the
censorship of stage plays (The Lord Stonham): *agreed* to.'[1]

Apart from the less dramatic dealings with the Lord Chamberlain's
office, the Royal Court had some rather larger confrontations which
greatly helped to point up the absurdity of pre-production censorship
of the stage and finally to bring about the investigation of the Joint
Committee on Censorship of the Theatre which led to the abolition
of the Lord Chamberlain's power over the theatre.

In 1966, theatre censorship was still operating under the authority
of the Theatres Act of 1843, under which the Lord Chamberlain was
given absolute authority to determine what could and what could not
be put upon any stage in Great Britain. There had been studies by
Select Committees of the House of Commons — on 1853, 1866, and
1892 — but they were concerned with his licensing of theatres rather
than with censorship of plays and no changes in the law were
recommended. In 1909 there was a Joint Selection Committee
examination of the whole question, including censorship and, among
other recommended changes, the Committee suggested that the
Lord Chamberlain's grounds for refusing to license a play should be
codified. The Committee said that the Lord Chamberlain should be
able to refuse a licence only if a play submitted might reasonably be
held: (a) to be indecent; (b) to contain offensive personalities; (c) to
represent on the stage in an invidious manner a living person, or any
person recently dead; (d) to do violence to the sentiment of religious
reverence; (e) to be calculated to conduce to crime or violence; (f) to
be calculated to impair friendly relations with any foreign power; (g)
to be calculated to cause a breach of the peace. The 1909 Report was
not adopted by the Government, but would have meant little change
if it had been. The recommendations for codifying the Lord
Chamberlain's rights of refusal to license were so vague as to be practically useless. However, although there were four more attempts to
introduce bills to deal with censorship between 1909 and 1966, it was
the criteria of the 1909 Select Committee which largely guided the
Lord Chamberlain in 1966.

Thus, in 1966 the operative law was still the Theatres Act of 1843.
Section twelve of the Act required the submission to the Lord
Chamberlain of any new stage play or addition to an old play intended to be produced or acted for hire in Great Britain seven days
before it was due to be first acted and made it an offence to present or

act for hire on the stage any play which had not been given a licence by the Lord Chamberlain. The penalty was a fine of up to £50, and the courts also had the power to deprive the theatre of its licence. Section sixteen provided that an actor was acting for hire if 'Any money or other reward shall be taken or charged, directly or indirectly', or if 'the purchase of any article is made a condition of admission' into the theatre to see the play, or if the play was acted 'in any house, room or place in which distilled or fermented excisable liquor' was sold. In addition to the provision for prior censorship of new plays[2] and for preventing or stopping the performance of any new plays or parts of new plays that had been disallowed, the Lord Chamberlain also had the general power to forbid any play or part of a play for any length of time, or absolutely, if, in his opinion, 'it is fitting for the preservation of good manners, decorum, or of the public peace' so to do. That provision conferred an unrestricted power upon the Lord Chamberlain to stop plays, whether new or old; albeit, it had long been held that performances in club theatres were exempt from his power – a subject which will be dealt with in some detail later in this chapter. The Lord Chamberlain also had always regarded action, or business, and dress as integral parts of the play and, therefore, subject to his control.

The administration of the licensing provision of the Theatres Act of 1843 was carried out by the Lord Chamberlain and his staff as part of their general duties. They were assisted by four examiners attached to the office on a part-time basis who received a statutory fee of two guineas for each full-length play read and one guinea for each one-act play. When an examiner read a play he would write a synopsis and conclude with recommendations. The synopsis and, when deemed necessary, the play would then be read by a member of the permanent staff – usually the Assistant Comptroller – who would comment on the recommendations of the examiner and add his own recommendations. The papers would then be reviewed by the Lord Chamberlain, who gave his decision. Whenever a difficult play was involved, or material cuts were in question, the Lord Chamberlain invariably read the play and frequently discussed it with the permanent staff and examiners. The decisions of the Lord Chamberlain were conveyed to the applicant by the Assistant Comptroller, who was available to discuss them with those concerned. The final decision, however, rested with the Lord Chamberlain and from his decision there was no appeal.

Inspection of productions was not frequent and depended on the assessment occasionally of a difficult play or resulted from complaints from members of the public.

This, then, was the system under which the English Stage Company produced its experimental new plays which attempted to deal seriously with contemporary problems. It was usually a workable system, for the Lord Chamberlains under which the Royal Court operated, the Earl of Scarborough until 1963 and Lord Cobbold thereafter, were widely thought to be fair and benevolent under the existing law. But pre-censorship was an anomaly – no other artistic endeavour had pre-censorship, and a play banned from the stage could be seen by millions on television or heard over the radio. A look at the Royal Court's dealings with the Lord Chamberlain show that, benevolent or not, his judgements were often absolutely absurd. In the light of later, post-censor audience reactions at the Royal Court and at the theatre in general, it became obvious that neither of the Lord Chamberlains represented even the conservative taste of the community and were hopelessly behind the times.

One early production by the English Stage Company pointed up the often ridiculous positions taken by the Lord Chamberlain. When *Fin de Partie* received its world première, in French, at the Royal Court in April 1957, no objections were raised to it by the Lord Chamberlain. However, when the play was submitted to him a year later in English. he found parts of it blasphemous and insisted upon alterations. Beckett agreed to some changes, but to others he was obdurate. After six months of negotiations the main point was resolved – to the satisfaction of the Lord Chamberlain, if not entirely satisfying to the English Stage Company or Beckett. In the scene in which Hamm, Clov, and Nagg all pray to God and then give up, Hamm was forbidden to say, 'The bastard! He doesn't exist!' Instead, the Lord Chamberlain accepted, 'The swine!' as somehow or other less offensive. And, of course, it must be assumed that, to the Lord Chamberlain's mind at least, all people who understand the French language were either incorruptible or beyond the hope of moral protection.

Another major obstruction occurred in 1957 when the English Stage Company submitted Ronald Duncan's *The Catalyst* to the Lord Chamberlain. The play deals with a triangle in which it is slowly discovered by the husband that he is the catalyst which has drawn the two women into a love relationship, though not clearly a physical one. Because it dealt with homosexuality, the Lord Chamberlain banned the play *in toto*. It is difficult today to see the reasoning behind that ban unless it is because the play shows no social consciousness and no judgement that the final arrangement among the three characters is 'evil'.

The suggestion was made to turn the Royal Court into a private 'club' theatre for the production of *The Catalyst*, thus, supposedly, escaping the Lord Chamberlain's authority. This attempt at circumvention was not without precedent.

The device of using a club theatre to get around the Lord Chamberlain was first used by the Shelley Society, formed in 1886 principally to produce Shelley's play *The Cenci*, which had been deemed unfit for public consumption by the Lord Chamberlain. In May of that year the Society gave a private matinée performance to which members were invited. The Shelley Society tack was taken by several other producing societies, most important of which was the Stage Society. In time, permanent club theatres were established. Although they were operating in open defiance of the Lord Chamberlain, he allowed them to continue. J. T. Grein opened his Independent Theatre in 1891 with a production of Ibsen's *Ghosts* and, although there were public demands that the play be stopped, and it had been banned previously, Grein was assured by the Lord Chamberlain that the play officially did not exist, as long as the performance remained a legally private one for members of the society and their guests. The precedent was established. Club theatres were often formed thereafter and were looked upon favourably by the Lord Chamberlains. In 1965 Lord Cobbold, the Lord Chamberlain, said:

> 'So long as they are genuine clubs for a genuine purpose I am very much in favour of theatre clubs. They give selective and interested audiences a chance to see experimental work and I think they are very useful to the theatre. Whether or not they could strictly be brought under the Lord Chamberlain's jurisdiction – which has never actually been tested in the courts – my predecessors and I have never wished to interfere with genuine theatre clubs.'

But he continued ominously:

> 'Where a management uses them for a different purpose, e.g., to put on for a long run a play part of which has been refused a licence, I think rather a different position arises. The arrangement is then really being used more as an attempt to evade the law . . . I can think of circumstances in which the Lord Chamberlain as custodian of the Theatres Act would feel it his duty to challenge the arrangement and to test the law in the courts. I very much hope myself that managements will have the good sense not to force the issue to this point, which might well involve difficulties for all theatre clubs and which would, in my view, be harmful to the general interests of the theatre.'[3]

In 1965 that was clearly a warning to the English Stage Company, but in 1957 there was no question of the Lord Chamberlain interfering with the club production of *The Catalyst*. George Devine had thought it would confuse the public if the Royal Court were to be turned into a club theatre at that early stage of the Company's history and the play was presented at the Arts Theatre Club on 25 March 1958, produced in association with the English Stage Company. It is interesting to note that in 1963 the Lord Chamberlain granted a licence for *The Catalyst* and it was then presented in the West End without any alteration to the text.

All of John Osborne's plays except *A Bond Honoured* were subjected to changes at the Lord Chamberlain's behest. The alterations were usually limited to word cuts. In *The Entertainer* some of the more puzzling excisions were 'ass-upwards', 'pouff', and 'camp'; and in *The World of Paul Slickey* (1959) he objected to the words, 'crumpet', 'queer', and 'fairy', among others. As a result of complaints received, the Lord Chamberlain ordered an inspection of the latter play at Leeds and subsequently demanded several changes. Among them he pointed out a line in the Income Tax Song, 'He's almost definitely queer', and said that the line must be totally eliminated and that no substitute referring to the Income Tax Inspector as homosexual would be allowed. In addition, he pointed out that his authority extended over stage business as an integral part of the play and that there had been deviations from the licensed business:

'The stage directions at the commencement ... are not observed. Jack is lying on top of Deidre, instead of sitting on the bed. When he moves himself Jack's shirt is seen to be outside his trousers, and the later dialogue is punctuated by his stuffing it back. Deidre's slip remains outside the whole time.

'*Requirement:* Jack and Deidre must sit on the bed as allowed. Jack must be fully clothed, not in *déshabillé*, and Deidre's slip must be inside her breeches.'[4]

When the Lord Chamberlain demanded fourteen cuts in *Luther* in 1961 Osborne at first refused to make any of them. The English Stage Company initially considered turning the Royal Court into a club theatre for the production, but after two weeks of negotiations the Lord Chamberlain withdrew all but four of his objections, which Osborne reluctantly agreed to accept.

In *The Blood of the Bambergs* (1962), three names were changed because the Lord Chamberlain thought they sounded too much like existing royal names, and 'Gentlemen at Arms' had to be changed to 'Halberdiers at Arms' because a group called 'Gentlemen at Arms' existed at Court. In addition, a film in which the Archbishop was seen but not heard was substituted for a speech.

Although seven passages were questioned in *Under Plain Cover*, presented on the same bill with *The Blood of the Bambergs*, the central sado-masochistic situation of a brother and sister innocently living in an incestuous union – and enjoying it – was allowed.

The Lord Chamberlain requested twenty cuts in *Inadmissible Evidence* in 1964, all related to taboos on language and reference to sexual practice; for example, 'arse' had to be changed to 'bum', and in 'Do you have it off with that girl of yours?' the dropping of 'off' somehow made it perfectly acceptable.

Also in 1964, Osborne's *A Patriot for Me* was submitted to the censor in the usual way. This time, however, the changes and cuts required were so extensive and damaging to the play that both Osborne and the English Stage Company found them entirely impracticable. On the grounds that the play was 'liable to corrupt', the Lord Chamberlain demanded the following cuts:

| | |
|---|---|
| *Act I, scene 1:* | 'His spine cracked in between those thighs. Snapped ... all the way up.' |
| *Act I, scene 4:* | the scene could not be played with the couple both in bed, and directions calling for one couple to watch another couple making love in a whorehouse (off-stage) were not allowed; |
| *Act I, scenes 5 and 7:* | reference to 'clap' and 'crabs': |
| *Act I, scene 10:* | this whole scene, in which Redl, the central character, has just had his first homosexual affair, must be deleted; |
| *Act II, scene 1:* | the entire scene, the drag ball, must be deleted (although men dressed in drag and performing actions with highly homosexual overtones could be seen by any child in most Christmas pantomimes); |

*Act III, scene 1:* the two men could not be in bed together, and other lengthy dialogue cuts;

*Act III, scene 2:* 'You were born with a silver sabre up your what-not' had to go;

*Act III, scene 4:* 'Tears of Christ!' was to be cut;

*Act III, scene 5:* the entire scene was to be deleted.[5]

Clearly, if all the changes and deletions requested by the Lord Chamberlain were made, the sensitive, genuinely beautiful play that had been written would have been destroyed. It was therefore decided in the autumn of 1964 to turn the Court into a 'club' theatre and to produce *A Patriot for Me* under the auspices of the English Stage Society in order to escape the power of the censor.

The English Stage Society agreed to present the production on the terms that the Company would be responsible for the production, theatre, cast, and staff. the Society would reimburse the Company to the extent of the net box office receipts after deducting the Society's advertising and other expenses, and the Society would receive ten per cent of the Company's future exploitation of the play, after deducting any loss on the original production. The Arts Council was approached and gave their assurance that their grant to the Company would not be changed during the limited time the theatre was operated as a 'club', and Alfred Esdaile, as licensee of the theatre, gave his permission for the play to be performed at the Court under club conditions. Although there were vague threats of intervention from the Lord Chamberlain's Office, the plans for the production went ahead. The Royal Court repeatedly issued statements that it did not intend its actions to be a challenge to the Lord Chamberlain and that it could only present the play if he agreed to the conditions. English Stage Society associate membership was offered for five shillings and total Society membership jumped to over 10,000 during the run of the play.

None of the major critics found the play to be a 'corrupting in-fluence'. Ronald Bryden, then critic for the *New Statesman*, pointed out the artistic fallacy of the Lord Chamberlain's stand:

'If anyone still doubts that art knows better than censorship, John Osborne's new play ... should provide clinching evidence. With the excision of this ballroom scene, for which it will clearly go down in theatrical history, the Lord Chamberlain apparently might have considered licensing *A Patriot for Me* for public per-formance. Apart from the fact that it is one of the best things Osborne has written, the deletion would have been ludicrously self-defeating ... Without its climatic evocation of high Hapsburg queerdom at its annual drag ball, *A Patriot for Me* would be, more or less, a sentimental high-flown piece of propaganda for the rights of a noble and oppressed minority. Osborne's ball scene is not only magnificently theatrical, the best thing in his play, but its centre, its validation, the image from which all else takes perspective and completeness.'

The play was a critical success and showed new developments in Osborne's talent – *The Times* said:

'The voraciousness of that talent is unequalled in the post-war theatre: where other playwrights have settled into fixed styles or mere professionalism, Osborne's work has grown away from the narrowly personal without losing its original fire.'

But the production *could not* be financially successful. It was an extremely expensive production – there were eighty-seven characters demanding thirty-seven actors and four musicians, all in period costumes – and the run had to be limited to just over six weeks. Although *A Patriot for Me* played to ninety-four per cent of financial capacity, there was a loss of over £15,000 on the production, of which Osborne himself bore half. If the play had not been banned by the Lord Chamberlain it would have been transferred into a larger West End theatre where it would probably have earned a profit. Thus, the case of *A Patriot for Me* provides a telling example not only of artistic meddling, but also of censorship depriving a playwright of his property without usual process of law and without appeal.

While *A Patriot for Me* was still running, the Royal Court submitted Edward Bond's *Saved* to the Lord Chamberlain for approval. He advised the Company that he would not allow the play to be performed before the general public unless substantial cuts were made to the script. The Company considered that it would be impossible to ask the author to make the required cuts and, after consulting with the Lord Chamberlain's Office again, felt that there was no hope of any compromise being reached. *Saved* had been chosen to open the Repertory Season in early October and William Gaskill suggested that performance of *Saved* should be given to the English Stage Society members only – thus making the Royal Court a 'club' theatre for that particular play – and that it should run in repertory with the other plays for which the general public could gain admittance.

The Arts Council, Alfred Esdaile, and the Greater London Council (by whom the theatre was licensed) were asked and again gave permission to operate as a 'club' theatre, and preparations began for the production. It was decided to open the season with the other two plays in the first part of the repertory – Ann Jellicoe's *Shelley* and N. F. Simpson's *Cresta Run* – and to bring *Saved* in third. It was announced that the Company was putting on *Saved* for the benefit of the English Stage Society members, who then numbered over 10,000 and to whom the Company felt a special responsibility.

*Saved* opened on 11 November 1965, and did indeed shock the critics and at least part of the general audience – as it was meant to do. *Saved* explores the brutality and emptiness of South London louts in a portrayal of cultural emptiness and the beastliness that is the result. Bond's brilliant ear for the working-class idioms was appreciated by the critics, but it was not – as it is not in reality – gentle and certainly not 'polite'. But the scene which really shocked the audience and to which the Lord Chamberlain had objected without compromise, involved the murder of a bastard baby in its pram by a group of layabouts, including its father. They spat upon it, pulled its hair, pinched it, and rubbed its face in its own excrement in a rising state of excitement before finally stoning it to death. B. A. Young, critic for *The Financial Times*, expressed one curious, but highly representative, view when he said:

'Perhaps I ought to be more concerned with the sinister under-current of South London life that drives girls into casual inter-course without a word of protest from their complaisant parents, and prompts boys to amuse themselves by stoning babies to death. I can only plead that I have lived a comparatively sheltered life, and if such things are really going on in South London they are properly the concern of the police and the magistrates rather than the audience of theatres, even the Royal Court.'

Young's outcry against going to the limits of brutality and his strange desire to play the ostrich was reflected by most of his colleagues. But Alan Brien of *The Sunday Telegraph* did not agree and brilliantly argued his stand:

'It appears that the British audiences and critics can stomach un-limited helpings of torture, sadism, perversion, murder and bestiality when perpetrated by foreigners upon foreigners in the past ... But when Edward Bond in *Saved* at the Royal Court shows us London youths, here and now, beating and defiling a bastard baby ... then a cry goes up to ban and boycott such criminal libels on our national character.

'Is it thought that such things cannot happen in this gentle and civilized land? Art and life have a way of reflecting each other in an eternity of mirrors and there is nothing that can be pictured even in the most grotesque of imaginations that has not been done by somebody somewhere sometime ...

'The action tests out Blake's epigram – 'Sooner murder an in-fant in its cradle than nurse unacted desires' – by carrying it to its extreme ... How does a human life weigh in the balance against egotistical satisfaction?

'He [Bond] gives no answers. From the general reception of his play, few people can bear even hearing the question. *Saved* makes an unsympathetic, disturbing, wearing, sometimes boring evening in the theatre. But I believe it fulfils one of the basic func-tions of the drama far better than *The Investigation* – that of making us remember the monster behind the mask on every one of us.'

The Lord Chamberlain was apparently in the majority who did not want the question asked. Police, acting on behalf of the Lord Chamberlain's Office, visited the theatre on 13 December and, although they were Society members, they were not made to show their membership cards. A summons was duly issued against the English Stage Company and in particular against William Gaskill as Artistic Director and Alfred Esdaile as licensee of the theatre. Clearly a test case of historic importance was to be initiated by the Lord Chamberlain. Although it was traditionally assumed that a club theatre was immune from the powers of the Lord Chamberlain, that belief had never been tested because no club theatre performance had ever been prosecuted. It appeared that the Lord Chamberlain, as he had suggested he might, was going to test that belief.

The prosecution, however, chose not to attack club theatres in general. Seemingly the Lord Chamberlain was gunning for the Royal Court as an *avant-garde* theatre as a result of complaints from pressure groups which were forcing him to take action. In the face of increased liberalism, the Lord Chamberlain prosecuted the English Stage Company on the grounds that the English Stage Society was only a front and that *Saved* was not being presented as a *bona fide* club production. On 14 February 1966, in front of Leo Gradwell, magistrate at the Marlborough Street Magistrates' Court, Oliver Nugent for the prosecution took the tack that a member of the Lord Chamberlain's staff had attended a performance of *Saved* and, although he had joined the Society, he was not required to show his membership card either when purchasing a ticket or when purchasing a drink at the theatre bar. With further evidence of police entering without showing cards, he intended to prosecute purely on the grounds that the production was not for club members only. He further stated: 'Perhaps I should point out that whether the Lord Chamberlain is right or wrong, or whether you think, or anybody else thinks, that this play should not, or should, be shown is entirely irrelevant to this case.' The prosecution further requested that all performances of *Saved* be stopped immediately, but John Gower, defending Gaskill, Esdaile, and Greville Poke, Secretary of the English Stage Company, said that his clients' case was that the Royal Court *was* a *bona fide* club, that the performances were lawful and would therefore continue.

On 7 March, the defence called Sir Laurence Olivier as witness on behalf of the English Stage Company. He gave his home address and then was asked his occupation.

'I am an actor, sir,' he replied.

He then said:

'The English Stage Company, in combination with the English Stage Society, which is its support group, has, I think, without any questions in the minds of anyone in my profession, been of the most vital value for the last ten years. Its chief aim has been to be a workshop for the dramatist. This aim carries with it as well a unique advantage for the dramatist as well as for the producer, actor, and designer.'

He then read a list of playwrights – including John Osborne, Samuel Beckett, Arnold Wesker, N. F. Simpson, Nigel Dennis, Eugène Ionesco and John Arden – who had been either discovered by the Company, or whom the Company had presented in Britain for the first time, or 'at least promoted and developed to a very high degree. They have good cause to think that the English Stage Company has provided them with a good turning point in their careers.' He also mentioned directors William Gaskill, Anthony Page, Lindsay Anderson, and Tony Richardson who had developed with the Company, and actors Alan Bates, Robert Stephens, Albert Finney, Peter O'Toole, Kenneth Haigh and actresses Rita Tushingham, Joan

Plowright, and others who owed a great deal to the Company. He continued:

> 'In addition, many performers have been able to take "post-graduate courses" with the Company. Dame Peggy Ashcroft, Rex Harrison, Sir Alec Guinness, and myself feel an enormous debt of gratitude to the English Stage Company for providing us with a new type of work. It altered entirely the colour and tone of my career at a time when it was becoming dangerously a little bit more staid, a little bit more predictable. I shall always be grateful that they gave me opportunities to show myself in other colours.'

In spite of Olivier's testimony and testimony by Lord Harewood and Norman Collins, Director and Deputy Chairman of A.T.V., to the effect that Society membership was strictly enforced, the magistrate found against the Royal Court, fined the Company costs of £50, and gave Gaskill, Esdaile, and Poke conditional discharges – a small penalty because he found them guilty only on a technicality of the law. He declared that the decision had nothing to do with the Society or its members, and added that he thought that the Company had been as careful as one could expect them to be about tickets and that everybody connected with the Society was 'perfectly splendid'. Gradwell stressed that his decision was based purely on the law, and the law stated that the Lord Chamberlain had authority over club theatres as well as public theatres. Gradwell said, 'The Act says nothing about societies. I am sitting on the rock of a statute and inviting you to rescue me from it. The law may be very unsatisfactory ... This case will probably result in a way that nobody wanted.' He found that the Theatres Act of 1843 did not stipulate that the play need be presented for the public, but only that it be presented for hire in order to fall under the authority of the Lord Chamberlain. He thought that a rich man who hired actors to perform an uncensored play for himself alone would bring himself within the statute. The prosecution had said that if the play had been presented by a *bona fide* theatre club, no offence would have been committed, and the defence had said the same thing. But the magistrate had said they were both wrong – that the English Stage Society *was* a *bona fide* club, but that still an offence had been committed because the play had been produced for hire – club or no club. So the whole basis of club theatres' presentation of uncensored plays had been undermined – something which the Lord Chamberlain had made clear he had not intended to do.

After the decision was given, Gaskill said, 'The whole theatre will be up in arms about this. Now the pressure against the Lord Chamberlain will mount.'

Alfred Esdaile said, 'The Lord Chamberlain has signed his own death warrant. He has done a stupid thing. The opposition against him will be tougher than ever before.'

Pressure had already mounted against the Lord Chamberlain. On 17 February 1966, while the *Saved* case was in adjournment for three weeks, Lord Annan, then Provost of King's College, Cambridge, had moved in the House of Lords to set up a joint committee of enquiry into the law and practice of stage censorship. He had pointed out that plays banned on the stage could be performed on television and that sketches about living people were seen on B.B.C. He had said that nudity and mime, which would not be likely to be passed by the Lord Chamberlain in the theatre, were permitted in ballet. The stage was censored, but not the music hall; nor were the strip-tease joints in Soho. 'To dramatists it must often appear that the more serious a play, the more likely it was to be censored.' Lord Annan also had pointed out the two basic principles upon which censorship was opposed: first, a man's work and his property could be destroyed without recompense and without appeal; and, second, censorship violated freedom of expression. He had also pointed to some of the absurd workings of censorship early in the century when three plays of Shaw had been banned, as were Ibsen's *Ghosts*, Granville-Barker's *Waste*, Sophocles' *Oedipus Rex*, and even *The Mikado* (for fear of offending a visiting Japanese prince). He had also pointed out the danger of having a censor dictate the kind of language to be used in the theatre:

> 'The day of the jewelled epigram is past and whether one likes it or not one has moved into the stern puritanical era of the four-letter word. There is a slight danger that the language of gentility may be imposed upon dramatists who are sincerely trying to evoke the manners and modes of different classes in society.'

Lord Annan had had no trouble finding support for his motion. Lord Gardiner, the Lord Chancellor, had attacked the whole system of pre-censorship for the stage and had asked:

> 'I wonder if someone will tell us where there is any other country in the world where there is pre-censorship of plays? How is it that the adults of all other countries can exist with a theatre which is free and subject only to the same laws of obscenity, blasphemy, and sedition as we have, and it is only grown-up Englishmen who have to have their plays read by somebody else beforehand who will decide whether they will be allowed to see them or not?'

The Earl of Scarborough, who had been Lord Chamberlain from 1953 to 1963, had said that he agreed it was time for another look at the problem, but he did not think it politic to do away with censorship altogether. He had said there was quick money to be made from obscenity and the representation of cruelty on the stage and, although he would not suggest that the theatre in its fullest sense would be lured by that, he had no doubt that some persons would be so lured. He had said that in exercising censorship he had tried to keep not too far away from the centre of public opinion, but he had found that very difficult in practice. Public opinion often did not exist, and if it did usually came too late.

Lord Cobbold also operated in accordance with his own view of public opinion. The previous year he had said:

> 'My personal objective is to try to assess the norm of educated,

adult opinion and if possible to keep just a touch ahead of it. I find I have to make a positive effort to keep my own personal tastes, likes and dislikes right out of the picture. They are obviously irrelevant for censorship purposes.'

He, too, had felt that it was time to examine theatre censorship, and for three reasons. First, the development of films, broadcasting, and television and the increasing scope of drama in those media made a new look at censorship of the theatre imperative. While there should not be a uniform code of censorship, he had said, it was absurd that the theatre was completely separated by Parliament. Secondly, he had agreed that the powers of censorship should not be held by any one man with no provision for appeal. Thirdly, he had doubted whether the responsibility for stage censorship should rest with the same man who was the head of the Queen's household. He did, however, think that censorship over the stage should be maintained in some form.

The debate had thus already started when the *Saved* case was decided on 1 April 1966 and the magistrate's decision made action all the more imperative. The escape valve of the club theatres for the production of uncensored plays could be closed at the Lord Chamberlain's will.

Lord Cobbold, however, apparently did not want the escape valve closed. After the *Saved* case the English Stage Company put on two more plays at the Royal Court which had been banned by the censor – van Itallie's *America Hurrah* in August 1967, and Charles Woods' *Dingo* in November 1967 – with no interference by the Lord Chamberlain's Office, although he would not permit *America Hurrah* to transfer to the Vaudeville Theatre after it had played its scheduled four weeks at the Court.

In June 1967, the Joint Committee on Censorship of the Theatre submitted its report. Three alternatives had been considered: continuation of compulsory pre-censorship, voluntary pre-censorship, and the abolition of pre-censorship. The findings of the Joint Committee had led them to recommend the last choice:

'The effect of the recommendations of the Committee will be to allow freedom of speech in the theatre subject to the overriding requirements of the criminal law which generally speaking applies to other forms of art in the country. The anachronistic licensing powers of the Lord Chamberlain will be abolished and will not be replaced by any other form of pre-censorship, national or local. The theatre will be subjected to the general law of the land, and those presenting plays which break the law will be subjected to prosecution under the relevant procedure. The penalities for offences will be realistically severe, but the author and producer will have the right to defend themselves before a jury and to plead the defence of artistic merit. Political censorship of any kind will cease.'

In October 1967, before a bill to abolish censorship had been introduced into the House of Commons, the Royal Court received another play which it had commissioned from Edward Bond – *Early*

*Morning.* Although opinions varied as to its meaning, the majority of
the Artistic Committee felt that it showed new development of Bond
as a writer and was an exciting experimental work which should be
seen. Oscar Lewenstein wanted to know what the chances were of
getting a licence from the Lord Chamberlain and Gaskill said that he
thought it would be a waste of time to apply for a licence as he knew
that Bond would not make any suggested cuts. Greville Poke,
however, pointed out that the Company had never presented a play
before without first submitting it and that the situation would be unknown if that were done. It was finally decided to submit the play to
determine its legal position.

Gaskill had been right in his assumption that submitting the script
of *Early Morning* to the Lord Chamberlain would be a waste of time,
but Edward Bond was not given a chance even to consider making
changes. For the first time since *The Catalyst* in 1957 a Royal Court
script was banned *in toto.* The reason was not primarily obscenity,
but rather that it portrayed Queen Victoria ('Call me Victor') in a les-
bian relationship with Florence Nightingale and was otherwise
irreverent to the Royal Family and the 'recently dead'.

The Arts Council was approached for permission to turn the Court
into a club theatre for the production of *Early Morning,* but this time
they refused to assent. The Arts Council, Joe Hodgkinson said, had
noted the decision of the magistrate in the *Saved* court case and the
claim that the Royal Court was a *bona fide* club had no relevance in
the context of the case and did not protect the Company from being
prosecuted for contravening the 1843 Theatres Act. The Arts Council said that if they gave their permission for *Early Morning* to be
presented they would be a party to the same offence. Permission had
not been asked for the presentation of *America Hurrah* as it had been
presented at the Court by an outside management, so the application
for *Dingo* had been the first to be made after the *Saved* case. It was
only after permission had been given to present *Dingo* as a club
production, said Hodgkinson, that the Arts Council had become
aware of the full implications of the judgment involving the 1843 Act.
If it had had the facts of the case before the *Dingo* application, permission would also have been refused for that. Lord Goodman,
Chairman of the Arts Council, had approached Lord Cobbold, the
Lord Chamberlain, to find out just what his attitude was towards
club productions. Lord Cobbold had intimated that he had no intention of changing his attitude and that he would permit certain club
theatres to do plays which need not have his licence as the 'escape-
hatch' of the *avant-garde* theatre. However, he had said, this was a
concession on his part and it was always to be understood that his
jurisdiction did extend over club theatres and he might even demand
certain alterations to the text of a club performance. He had said that
he himself was not concerned with the magistrate's decision; that
was a legal matter merely emphasizing that his power extended to all
plays where artists engaged for hire.

Arts Council permission was required because their grant was
made on the basis of the policy statement submitted annually by the
English Stage Company, and part of that stated policy was that the
Royal Court was a public theatre.

Gaskill said that it was also Company policy to present certain experimental plays and in the history of the Company there had been trouble over many of the plays that had been presented. Writers were writing plays which could not be licensed by the Lord Chamberlain, but those plays should still be produced. He thought that when the Royal Court could not put on new plays, and not certainly the most important new plays, then the English Stage Company would cease to have any real function.

The Arts Council, nevertheless, determined to withhold its grant for the period of the run of *Early Morning*.

Gaskill's interpretation of the Arts Council's immovable stand against *Early Morning* was that they didn't want the play done. George Strauss, M.P., had a bill to abolish theatre censorship ready to be introduced in the House of Commons and its passage was all but assured. The Arts Council had worked long and hard for the defeat of censorship of the theatre and they were afraid that the production of *Early Morning* might hurt the bill's chances of passage. It was not, in Gaskill's opinion, that they disapproved of the play, but that they were afraid of what public reaction against it could do at that particular time.

Although the Arts Council had felt that it must, as a public body, withhold support for a clearly illegal act, it did not otherwise attempt to stop the production. Lord Goodman said that the Arts Council had no intention of making further hardship and that permission to put on *Early Morning* would not be refused if the English Stage Company could find another management or a private source of income that would pay for the production and the running costs, and the Arts Council would not object to the Company's using its accumulated reserves for the production.

The Royal Court found itself faced with a curious dilemma. The Arts Council move had forced the Company to withdraw *Early Morning* from the main bill, for the time being at least. The alternatives left open were to present the play as a 'Sunday Night' production, or to wait until the demise of the Lord Chamberlain's power over theatre – certainly no more than eleven months away – and present the play in the main bill in the normal way and with the normal subsidy. However – and here was the dilemma – once George Strauss's bill went through, the Company's position could be even more dangerous than before because it would then be subject to common law – and prosecution by a member of the public was fully expected. A successful prosecution under the common law would certainly result in far greater penalities than under the 1843 Theatres Act and would probably result in the loss of the theatre's licence. If the play were presented while the censor was still in power, the Company risked prosecution from him; if it were presented after the Lord Chamberlain lost his censorship powers, the Company faced public prosecution without the protection of the Lord Chamberlain from the common law. The position of freedom carried its dangers.

Gaskill had written to the Lord Chamberlain to find out what his position would be if *Early Morning* were put on by a club theatre, such as Hampstead. The Lord Chamberlain had replied that he would feel bound to pass the papers to the Director of Public

Prosecutions. In view of what he had been told in writing, Gaskill thought that the Lord Chamberlain might prosecute a 'Sunday Night' performance, but, on the other hand, the Lord Chamberlain had said verbally that he would not do so. It was decided to accept the lesser risk, and, rather than face the possibility of prosecution under the common law, to give *Early Morning* a 'Sunday Night' production to run for two consecutive Sundays, as was the usual procedure.

When the annoucement of the production was made, *The Times* headlined: 'GASKILL STRIKES AGAIN.'

But it was the police who struck. On the night of the first performance, 31 March 1968, they arrived and, after the performance was over, made inquiries and interviewed Gaskill, but made no threats. That show of interest, however, was enough threat for Alfred Esdaile (as licensee of the theatre), and at his insistence – overruling the Management Committee's wishes – the second club performance was cancelled, although the Court did present what it called a 'critics' dress rehearsal' on that date. Invited guests were allowed to enter through a side entrance only after being personally recognized and no charge for admission was made – thus putting the performance in a legal – if somewhat bizarre – position.

*Early Morning* was the last play banned by the Lord Chamberlain. On 28 September 1968, George Strauss's bill, the Theatres Act of 1968, became law and pre-censorship of theatre in Great Britain came to an end.

The loathsome effects of having theatre without pre-censorship apparently were not too shocking for the public, as had been feared by some. Even the Royal Court's fears of a rash of prosecutions against theatre management did not materialize – there has not yet been one prosecution. One of the first results of the demise of the censor was a short repertory season of Bond plays at the Royal Court – *Saved*, *Narrow Road to the Deep North*, and *Early Morning* – which opened on 7 February 1969, and ran until 12 April. Martin Esslin, in his review of *Saved* and *Narrow Road to the Deep North*, succinctly summed up the new post-censorship situation in *Plays and Players*:

'Nothing could have shown up the idiocy of British stage censorship in its declining phase than the reaction of the public – and even the critics! – to the revival of *Saved* at the Royal Court. After the grotesque antics in which the moral health of the nation was supposedly to be preserved by the imposition of a fine and the banning of the play, less than four years later it is staged, received with quiet respect and recognized to be a moral tract for the times, no less. Can anyone be proved to have been depraved or corrupted by it? Has it led to sadistic orgies? Or riots in the streets of Chelsea? Where, then, are all the arguments which maintained stage censorship in being for decades? 'Oh, well, old boy, if you allowed that sort of thing, who knows what might happen?' Well, now we know the answer. *Nothing* except that some people emerge from the theatre with a deeper insight, a greater compassion for the sufferings of some of their fellow human beings.'

Censorship of the stage had been under attack for generations before the English Stage Company had come into being, but, partly as a result of the Company's willingness to fight for its right to deal seriously with contemporary problems, the whole idea of theatrical censorship had finally become too obviously stupid to be allowed to continue. The abolition of censorship of the stage was simply a facing up to reality and the Theatres Act of 1968 allowed the whole of theatre to deal seriously with contemporary reality in an adult manner.

### Notes

1. *Joint Committee on Censorship of the Theatre Report,* Her Majesty's Stationary Office, 1967, p. iii. (Hereinafter referred to as *Joint Committee Report.*)
2. A play was considered 'new' if it was first presented after 22 August 1843, the date when the Act had come into force.
3. 'Censor Speaks,' *Sunday Times*, 11 April 1965.
4. Richard Findlater, *Banned! A Review of Theatrical Censorship in Britain* (MacGibbon and Kee, Ltd, 1967), p. 184. Quoting from the Lord Chamberlain's archives.
5. John Osborne, *A Patriot for Me*, Faber and Faber, 1965, p. 128.

# 5 October 1965 to August 1970

When William Gaskill, at the age of 34, accepted the position of Artistic Director of the English Stage Company in January 1965, he immediately began making plans for his first season. Although he didn't fill his new position officially until July, by April he had proposed that the Royal Court again form a permanent acting company and perform new plays in repertory, and the Management Committee had accepted the proposals. It was agreed to extend the Repertory Season for a period of six months, from October 1965 to the following April, and to employ twenty-one actors for the Company at pay ranging from £15 to £40 per week. At that rate the estimated loss would run at £72,192 for a full year, or £37,906 for the intended six months, based on the usual box office takings of fifty per cent of capacity.

The Arts Council studied the plans and estimates and sent their assurance to the Company that they were most sympathetic and encouraging towards the proposal. They accepted the documents *in toto* as being right in the context of the existing London theatrical scene and thought that the policy was right at the estimated level of cost, although they had some reservations as to whether the policy could actually be carried out at the figure given.

It was also decided to amend the standard author's contract to make it more fair to the playwright who would have his play in the repertory with no immediate prospect of a transfer into the more profitable West End. It was thus amended so that option money would be an outright payment instead of an advance on account of royalties and when the play was performed less than eight times a week at the Royal Court (as was bound to be the case under the repertory system) payment would be seven-and-a-half per cent of the gross for each performance up to the twenty-second performance, after which payment would rise to ten per cent of the gross. The twenty-first performance would also entitle the Company to full participation in the subsidiary rights of the play. The latter provision would allow for the eventual transfer of the play even though no immediate transfer could be arranged.

A company of actors was formed for the season, including Jean Boht, John Bull, Richard Butler, Timothy Carlton, John Castle, Frances Cuka, Iain Cuthbertson, Avril Elgar, Barbara Ferris, Lucy Fleming, Alison Frazer, Bernard Gallagher, Nerys Hughes, Kika Markham, Gwen Nelson, Ronald Pickup, Tony Selby, Sebastian Shaw, William Stewart, Dennis Waterman, and Frank Williams.

After the change of scheduling occasioned by the banning of *Saved*, the Repertory Season opened on 18 October 1965, with

*Shelley*, written and directed by Ann Jellicoe. Not one of the major critics liked the play. They all found it dull – a mixture of Victorian melodrama and documentary styles which neither gave a clear interpretation of the facts nor developed a sense of sympathy and interest in the characters.

On 28 October, N. F. Simpson's 'lunatic fantasy', *The Cresta Run*, opened as the second production. The critics again were in agreement that the central idea, a satire on espionage thrillers, was too thin to carry the comedy for a whole evening and that the Royal Court had another flop on its hands.

On 3 November, Bond's *Saved* joined the repertory. Again the critics attacked unmercifully, with the notable exceptions of Alan Brien in the *Sunday Telegraph* and Ronald Bryden in *New Society*, who said:

'Faced at the Royal Court with a skilful, indignant, and moving play by Edward Bond, the London press almost to a man has howled it down . . .

'What the majority has refused to see in this case (the majority of critics, that is – the second night audience, with whom we weeklies were invited, listened intently and applauded vehemently) is that *Saved* is a play about poverty in Britain now. True, it's difficult for most newspapers to recognize such poverty. Haven't they established that the poor are no longer with us . . .? How can anyone be poor in our affluent Zion of nylon, do-it-yourself coffee tables and £100,000 jackpots?

'Mr Bond is out to rub noses in the fact that the real new poor are the old poor plus television, sinking deeper in a form of poverty we do not yet recognize – poverty of culture. To us, the clerisy, 'poverty of ideas' is a term of individual blame, a schoolmaster's accusation of laziness and improvidence, as poverty of cash was to the Victorians. Mr Bond lays it as an actual deprivation at society's door, in all its stultifying and tragic consequences.'

But the majority of the critics were shocked by the play and said so in scathing reviews.

On 9 December, a revival of John Arden's *Serjeant Musgrave's Dance* was put into the repertory in a production directed by Jane Howell. When the same play had been produced at the Court in 1959 the critics had panned it so thoroughly that it had had to be taken off after twenty-eight performances, having made a loss greater than the Court's Arts Council grant for the whole year. In his review of the revival, Harold Hobson said that the 1959 production had 'provided an evening of such intolerable boredom that even today one yawns to think of it.' The revival, however, proved a success – mainly due to the acting of Iain Cuthbertson. Although not all the critics agreed, the majority opinion concurred with Peter Lewis of the *Daily Mail*, who said:

'This six-year-old classic – and, for all its warts, it must be hailed as such – has put the new Royal Court squarely on its mettle. Last night, for the first time this season, they began to look like more than an efficient repertory company.'

The box office, though better than for the other three plays in the repertory, proved disappointing. It met its budget, but did not prove successful enough to make up for the poor returns on the other plays.

The 1965 Christmas show was Keith Johnstone's Studio production of *Clowning* – presented as a lecture to get around the Lord Chamberlain's inability to pass improvisational work. *Clowning* was considered to be artistically successful, but, perhaps because it was presented in the afternoons only, sold only twenty-two per cent of seating capacity.

On 1 January 1966, Thomas Middleton's Jacobean comic satire, *A Chaste Maid in Cheapside*, opened and played to only fifty-two per cent of seating capacity. The reviews were mixed, but *The Times'* reaction was an unequivocal 'rave': 'This bawdy, realistic, and brilliantly directed comedy of Jacobean London is much the best thing that has appeared in the new Royal Court season.' But, though an artistic success, *A Chaste Maid in Cheapside* did not cover its budget.

*The Knack*, by Ann Jellicoe, was revived on 17 February, as part of the Court's policy of reviving plays which had failed to get proper recognition the first time the Court had presented them. Although it received generally good reviews, *The Knack*, too, fell well below the budgeted fifty per cent of financial capacity.

The final addition to the Repertory Season came on 6 March, with the production of two new one-act comic plays, *Transcending* by David Cregan and *The Performing Giant* by Keith Johnstone. The shorter *Transcending* received glowing reviews, but the main part of the evening, *The Performing Giant*, was crushingly panned on the most damning of grounds: it was found to be boring and unfunny.

In the six months from October 1965 to April 1966, the box office takings, at thirty-two per cent of financial capacity, had been well below average and the Company was in dire financial trouble. In October 1965, the Company had had a cash balance of £35,000, but by March 1966, it had lost £48,000; so the balance had been completely wiped out and the Company was entering the new financial year with an overdraft of approximately £4,000, having received a supplementary grant of £9,000 from the Arts Council for the year. It is difficult to say just how much of the box office reduction was directly attributable to playing in repertory. The absence of star names and the economy nature of some of the productions were contributory factors, though those factors do not necessarily go hand in hand with the repertory system.

In April 1966, Gaskill considered it best to revert to straight runs from the end of July, when the new repertory season was to end – unless by that time there was a marked increase in box office receipts. If that were to happen, he felt that the Company should consider a more limited form of repertory: two plays a week, rather than three, for shorter seasons of three to four months with gaps between for straight runs and, therefore, possible transfers. The increase in cost for the existing system of repertory had not been enormous, but if leading actors were to be imported from time to time and the lavishness of productions were to be increased, the costs would mount steeply and it seemed unlikely that there would be an immediate corresponding increase in the box office.

Gaskill thought it important to stress the advantages of the repertory system before rejecting it out of hand. The actual positive results of the first six months were seen to be: (1) an increase in advance bookings; (2) the nursing of *Saved* after unfavourable notices, which would not have been possible in the straight-run system; and (3) the beginnings of a regular audience. During the first six-month repertory period the box office takings were only thirty-two per cent of capacity, but the seats sold were forty-seven per cent. The fifteen per cent difference was partly due to ticket price reductions, but also to the fact that more of the audience, particularly the young, were buying the cheaper seats – which were often sold out even for an unsuccessful show. Discussions had been held after the performances of many of the plays and a new interest and excitement had been shown, particularly among those younger audiences.

The financial failure of the Repertory Season was caused by – in addition to the poor box office receipts – gross underestimation of both production costs and hires of costumes and rehearsal space, which were in fact nearly double that which had been estimated. Those costs would, of course, apply in either the straight-run or the repertory system. The actual increase in costs of the repertory system were in the technical staff necessary for changeovers, the changeovers themselves, and the carrying of a large company. The extra annual cost for maintaining the repertory system was estimated at:

|  | £ per week | Weeks | Total |
|---|---|---|---|
| Changeovers | 75 | 52 | 3,900 |
| Extra technical staff | 51 | 52 | 2,652 |
| Extra stage and electric | 15 | 52 | 780 |
| Increased company | 100 | 52 | 5,200 |
| Extra hires | 75 | 52 | 3,900 |
| Extra publicity | 30 | 52 | 1,560 |
|  |  |  | £17,992 |
| *Less:* Artists rehearsals | £4,000 |  |  |
| Show staff | 300 |  |  |
|  |  |  | 4,300 |
| Annual extra cost of repertory |  |  | £13,700 |

Because of the financial straits caused by the added costs and reduced income during the Repertory Season it was decided to change the policy – to revert to the earlier policy of Devine – and to mount eight productions, four of which would be revivals. The revivals were rehearsed for from six to eight weeks and played for eight weeks, and the four new plays were each rehearsed for four weeks and played for four weeks. (The revivals were given more weight because they were designed to provide the financial success needed to carry on the work with the new plays.) It was also deemed necessary to bring in stars whenever possible. Gaskill felt that working towards four major productions planned a year in advance would allow flexibility and give more time for work on a programme of 'Sunday Night' productions and on a reorganization of the script department, which would provide a new stimulus in the theatre.

N. V. Linklater said that the Arts Council would take into account the change of policy. Robin Fox pointed out to him that there was no policy change; that, in fact, the Company was really going back to what had been done before – producing four prop plays during the year. In February 1967, the Arts Council stated that it was not happy with the number of revivals and felt that the Company should do more new plays. Dennis Andrews said that, looking at it from the Arts Council's point of view, they could only justify the Company's grant if it were doing a programme of work that no other theatre in London was doing. The Arts Council did not expect the Company to mount a season of all new plays, but did wish the emphasis to be placed on finding and developing new playwrights. Andrews said that the English Stage Company was the only theatre getting something near the sum recommended by the Willet Report[1] and, because of that, the Arts Council was open to greater criticism in connection with the Royal Court than with any other theatre in the country. The Company's future programme included a number of importations, such as the Living Theatre, a production by Frank Dunlop, and a play by Charles Wood originally produced at Nottingham, instead of more new plays which originated at the Court and for which the grant was given.

Gaskill said that nine months earlier the Company had been under pressure to balance its accounts and it had done that, but only by doing revivals. He thought it would be possible to do a sustained programme of new and experimental plays, but that would mean rethinking the budget because an all-year-round programme of new plays should not be budgeted on more than thirty-five per cent of financial capacity. He also said that the alternative to the existing programme would be to do plays for three weeks with three weeks' rehearsal and a simplified set. The problem, then, was to present new plays cheaply without damaging the image or standards of the theatre, which were widely recognized to be very high.

Gaskill felt, following the discussion, that the Court's programme should be made more flexible. He thought it important to stir things up in organization of the theatre and as a step in that direction it had been decided to cancel the Frank Dunlop programme and in that eight-week gap to do a series of four plays, each for two weeks, on a budget limited to £1,604 per play.

It must be emphasized that during the whole of the discussion, the Arts Council, through Dennis Andrews, was not questioning the policy of the English Stage Company, with which it totally agreed, but was disturbed by what it felt to be deviations from that policy. It must also be emphasized that at no time did the Arts Council criticize the plays which the Royal Court had done or was planning to do; it felt concerned at the fact that they were not new plays originating at the Court and that was the limit of the criticism. Nor did the Arts

Council suggest what plays or kind of plays the Court should do in place of revivals and importations.

The 'new' policy was initiated by the production of *Ubu Roi* on 21 July 1966, starring Max Wall, famous as a music hall comedian, and with sets designed by David Hockney, the pop-art painter. Staged in pop-art scenery and science fiction costumes, the production was highly praised by the critics. After all, the play had been written in 1896, had influenced most of the playwrights since – particularly those working in the 'theatre of the absurd' genre – and yet had never before been given a professional production in England. Although most critics felt that the play had lost much of its shock effect and sting, they generally applauded the production and noted the social relevance and timeliness of the play. Nevertheless, box office takings again proved disappointing.

The next revival was Gaskill's production of *Macbeth*. When deciding to do *Macbeth*, Greville Poke, in a Management Committee meeting, had wondered if it was right to do a Shakespeare play because it would place the Court in competition with the Royal Shakespeare and the National Theatre, and the Court's budget would not provide for a large-scale production. Gaskill pointed out that there had been few productions of Shakespeare in London in the past few months and that any production at the Court would obviously have to be done in an original way. Jocelyn Herbert said that any director undertaking *Macbeth* would need a very clear vision of how to do the play and that the main difficulty lay in audiences being traditionally minded.

She was right. Although box office success was assured when Alec Guinness agreed to play Macbeth and Simone Signoret agreed to play Lady Macbeth, critical success was not assured. Gaskill's production was totally non-illusionistic and used many 'Brechtian' devices. The stage was brilliantly illuminated during the whole production – night never fell – and the set was of sandpaper, completely devoid of any relief or scenery and with only one entrance. There were no props except those which the actors took on and off. Above all, there was Lady Macbeth whose command of the English language was, to say the least, rather poor. After saying that the seats were nearly all sold by opening night, Milton Shulman of the *Evening Standard* launched his attack:

'It is probably a sad reflection on the theatre-going public's taste that they risked their money without caring what they were going to see. Guinness and Signoret announcing trains at Crewe might have achieved the same audience response.

'Relieved, therefore, of the responsibility of harming the box office, a critic feels more lighthearted than usual when he can solemnly announce that this *Macbeth* is the worst *Macbeth* that he has ever seen performed in the West End by a responsible theatrical company.

'The blame for this pretentious shambles must primarily belong to William Gaskill whose direction was so perverse, so insensitive, so precocious and so self-indulgent that it mangles into ludicrous strips one of our greatest plays.'

B. A. Young of the *Financial Times* disagreed only slightly: 'This may not be the worst *Macbeth* I have ever seen, but it is undoubtedly the dullest.' Simone Signoret's performance was seen as an absolute disaster. Those who could understand her at all found her rhythm wrong for blank verse and her French accent distracting. W. A. Darlington of the *Daily Telegraph* found the evening disappointing, but did think the production worth seeing. Only Harold Hobson gave unqualified praise to the production. He found it 'fascinatingly experimental' and said, 'Its most striking effects are such as would never, in fact could never, be found in any ordinary presentation of the play.' But Hobson was alone in his praise. With the exception of Darlington, the rest of the critics damned without mitigation.

Gaskill struck back. On 25 October he sent a condemning letter to the editors of all the major periodicals:

'Dear Sir,

Our production of *Macbeth* has produced a predictable crop of cheap journalism from the so-called critics of the national dailies. I am writing personally to all the critics, including yours, but the situation between the serious theatres and the newspapers has been deteriorating to such an extent recently that I feel I must write to you about this problem.

'I have always thought that no-one could doubt the seriousness of the intentions of the Royal Court Theatre, however critical they might be of some of its work. Our programme is planned in consultation with an artistic committee and with the full approval of the Arts Council.

'Our record in the last ten years is such that British theatre is now considered the best in the world. We are given a reasonable subsidy by the Arts Council to carry on this work but our financial position is constantly endangered by the flippancy of the theatre critics. I do not consider the work of a serious theatre to be a subject for sensational news items, which is all most critical notices amount to.

'The concept of the First Night with all that it entails – notices hurriedly written to catch a deadline, the need of the critic to make journalistic capital out of his notice – is destructive of serious work. It is notorious that the Broadway theatre, where the stress on the First Night and the subsequent notices is even greater, has failed to produce any new writing talent and that the commercial pressure on managements has strangled creative enterprise.

'The present vitality of the British theatre springs directly from the work of George Devine and his associates at this theatre – a work which I am proud to carry on. It would be sad if this vitality were threatened by a situation increasingly similar to the American one.

'In the circumstances, we are seriously considering whether we should invite your critic to future performances. This would be a grave step for any theatre to take but we feel the present level of criticism is so low as almost to warrant it.

'The only other solution would be to give critics the opportunity to reflect a little before writing their reviews and staggering their visits over several days, to avoid the appalling mass of them on a First Night.

'I realize that this will reduce the newsworthiness of their reports. I personally could not be more happy, but you as an editor might feel differently. I would welcome your comments.

Yours sincerely,
William Gaskill'

The critics' reactions were predictable. They found the letter rude and arrogant and Gaskill's position totally indefensible. Milton Shulman answered the charges in a thoughtful article. He found Gaskill's anger 'a natural reaction born of the wasted hours and effort that may have been summarily or pitilessly dismissed or derided.' But, continued Shulman:

'Since critics – whether the artist likes it or not – are merely a sample audience, a barometer of opinion, a middle man between the work and its goal, they are the obvious object of abuse if they report today what the public is likely to feel tomorrow.'

Shulman, as did the other critics, accused Gaskill of whining over poor reviews and forgetting the good reviews that had done so much to publicize the Company and its artists. They all pointed out that they were highly unlikely to change their opinions significantly even if they did revisit the production or take longer in writing their reviews. And, should a state-subsidized theatre be allowed to produce its work without comment, to allow only those critics who have only good things to say about it?

Gaskill, of course, had not complained about bad notices but about poor criticism – unserious, facile passing of judgement.

After writing his letter, Gaskill had gone to Tunisia for a holiday. The B.B.C. brought him back to face the critics in a televised discussion. Gaskill admitted that he had written the letter in anger, but said, 'I am not interested in your personal opinion; I am interested in how you reach it and how you educate your audience.' Although Harold Hobson said he was finding himself on Gaskill's side, the thirty-five minute discussion resolved nothing. As the chairman said, 'After all, none of us thought it would.'

When Gaskill asked Alec Guinness what he thought of the critics' reactions, he said, 'I never read the critics.' Gaskill told him about the row and why he had so suddenly returned from Tunisia. Guinness said, 'Silly boy. You've spoiled your holiday.'

The Council of the English Stage Company were not pleased with the whole business. However, after a meeting of the Management Committee there was no censure made – although the newspapers had spoken of the possibility of Gaskill's losing his job. The Committee did dissociate themselves from the statements and made it very clear that Gaskill was speaking only for himself and not for the Company. Although many members of the Committee agreed with Gaskill, at least in part, the critics would continue to receive invitations to first nights.

Guinness, while not entering into the dispute, did give his reasons for considering the production a success and, perhaps unconsciously, neatly explained the problem of reviewing experimental work at the Royal Court:

'The work I've been doing lately has been *lazy* work. It hasn't demanded things which might be above me. If I don't challenge myself this way *now*, I might never be able to. After all, I'm fifty-three now, and opportunities to stretch myself are going to be rarer in the future.

'I don't regret doing this [*Macbeth*] at all. There have been mistakes, of course. But I've learnt such a lot. You see, in this production, where there's hardly any set and the lights are blazing most of the time, everything is stripped down bare. You, the actor, are absolutely on your own. You cannot flick your little finger without it seeming as significant as a pistol shot. You can't be protected by lots of lush scenery.

'You see, none of us did this play for money or reputation or anything like that. I'm getting £30 a week for it and I don't expect Simone's getting much more than that. We did it for the gamble, for the excitement . . . Of course, the gamble didn't quite come off . . . But, you know, I have this feeling that this production may be seen some time in the future as being something quite germinal to a new approach to Shakespeare. You can't always go on what people feel at the time . . . Suppose one had told Picasso when he started: "Don't paint like that. Paint nice chocolate-box pictures. Birthday cards. That's what people want." If he had done so the future would have lost something.'[2]

Gaskill still thinks that critics are 'a terrible hindrance', that they judge the Royal Court productions by the same criteria they use for West End 'entertainment'. Although he realizes that there are serious critics, as well as those who approach their jobs with flippancy, his basic disagreement is with the whole idea of criticism:

'The critics have often been extremely friendly and they often fight for new writers. But, you see, all critics are concerned with evaluation and evaluation isn't what gets you an audience. Pleasure and experience are what an audience *should* go for; they don't, or shouldn't, go for evaluation (although I recognize that some do). An audience who actually go for the experience of theatre is the only audience worth having. But, whenever the critics attack a piece, they will say, "Well, I've given you, over the years, twenty good notices out of thirty," as if that were really what we're talking about.

'It's not what we're talking about at all . . .

'The critics should stop writing — become sociologists, learn what it's all about, learn that life can't be satisfied by a series of values.

'I think now it's essential to see things before critics have talked about them. If someone says that this actor says this line in this way, the impact can never be the same again when you go to see it.

They put their dead hand on everything; they do make the theatre something dead and tied up and put away.

'They're critics and what else can they do?'

After the Management Committee's announcement, the furore of the battle died down as abruptly as it had begun and the critics were at the Royal Court for the next production, *The Lion and the Jewel*, a new play by the Nigerian Wole Soyinka. Nearly all the critics liked the play and only Felix Barker of the *Evening News* referred to the recent dispute.

The critics were quick to forgive, but there is no doubt that the animosity has remained and occasionally erupts anew. If nothing else, the Royal Court's repeated attacks upon the critics and their personal values have made the critics less willing to champion the cause of the Court. They continue to remain outspoken and to act in their roles as 'a sample audience', pointing out what they find good and what they find not so good in the work of the Court. But there can be little doubt that the assaults upon them did nothing to help the cause of new drama. Of course nothing can remain as fresh and new once it has been described. But people will ask and surely the reviewers and critics are in a position to be asked. The best of them readily admit their prejudices – what theatregoer is for a moment unaware of Harold Hobson's predilection for French drama? – and very few people can attempt to see everything, no matter how much they may desire to do so. The general audience, and even the small regular audience at the Court, seek some guidance and the reviewers and critics attempt to provide intelligent guidance. Errors in judgement will be made, especially when dealing with new forms or unusual views expressed by the playwrights, but that does not mean that the reviewers should not express what they believe. The public must come to know the prejudices of the reviewers and count them in when making their personal decisions.

*The Lion and the Jewel* was followed by a revival of the long-neglected *The Soldier's Fortune* by Thomas Otway. Again, most of the critics found the production good and the choice worthwhile.

On 24 February 1967, Arnold Wesker's *Roots* was revived, partly to satisfy the demand for a schools' production. Chosen on the basis of a questionnaire circulated to schools in the London area, *Roots* was the first of several productions aimed at developing a young audience. Every night one hundred seats, spread throughout the house except in the upper circle, were set aside for students at five shillings each. In addition, there were six schools' matinees during the two-and-a-half week run of *Roots*. The production, a naturalistic collector's piece complete with the smells of cooking food, proved highly successful with critics, schools, and the general public alike.

On 16 March 1967, D. H. Lawrence's *The Daughter-in-Law*, written in 1911, was given its first public performance. Lawrence had written his first play, *A Collier's Friday Night*, in 1909 when he was twenty-four, and wrote two more plays, *The Daughter-in-Law* and *The Widowing of Mrs Holroyd*, in 1911 (Lawrence wrote eight plays altogether). But, like so many other writers, he had found publication much easier than achieving a theatrical production. It was this brilliant production of *The Daughter-in-Law* which led to Peter Gill's memorable productions of all three plays in the spring of 1968. At that time *The Widowing of Mrs Holroyd* had been last produced in 1926 and *A Collier's Friday Night* had been produced once – at the Court in a 'Sunday Night' production by Gill in 1966. After over half a century, D. H. Lawrence was discovered as a playwright, and one of worth, if not brilliance.

The new season, 1967–8, began with Gaskill's production of Chekhov's *Three Sisters* in a new version by Edward Bond. Gaskill surprised everyone by casting Marianne Faithfull, then a pop singer, as Irina – her first acting role. Gaskill was accused by an actor, Barry Schwartz, of having held mock auditions and of having cast Marianne Faithfull purely as a publicity gimmick. Gaskill, however, had auditioned sixty actresses in the normal way and had, in fact, offered the role to another actress first, but she had had to refuse the part because a repertory company would not release her from her contract. Gaskill responded to the allegations by saying, 'I suggest people making these claims should wait and see how good Marianne is.' The critics found her quite acceptable indeed. Irving Wardle of *The Times* said that, despite a few swallowed climaxes, she 'emerges as a recruit of startling emotional power.' The rest of the production, though some found it heavy and gloomy, was generally well received as interesting and pleasurable, if not great. Some critics took the trouble to compare Bond's version of the script with earlier versions and found it to be nicely sharpened in effect and very actable. The play was a popular success as well, playing to ninety per cent of seating capacity and seventy-five per cent of financial capacity and was thus partly responsible for rescuing the Company from its financial difficulties.

That financial recover was further buttressed in the summer of 1968 by the production of two new plays by John Osborne – *Time Present* and *The Hotel in Amsterdam* – and by the highly successful revival of *Look Back in Anger* in October 1968. Indeed, the continued loyalty of John Osborne to the theatre which gave him his first chance has long been one of the great assets of the Company. Osborne's loyalty is not, however, a compromising or cramping loyalty, as is evidenced by the season of his plays performed at the Greenwich Theatre, in December 1974.

Although in just over a year the Royal Court had produced six revivals, the theatre was not becoming a museum for old plays. The plays had been carefully chosen for social relevance and had been given original, experimental productions. The 'Sunday Night' productions, too, had continued and during that same period of time ten new plays had been produced (counting *The Daughter-in-Law*). One of the new plays, *When Did You Last See My Mother*, was written by Christopher Hampton when he was eighteen and, after playing for two Sundays at the Court, was transferred directly into the Comedy Theatre, making Hampton the youngest dramatist within living memory to have a play presented in the West End. His second play, *Total Eclipse*, was presented at the Royal Court in 1968. Since then Hampton has been attached to the Court, under an Arts Council grant, as resident dramatist and head of the script department. At the end of his first year he was offered a grant to be playwright-in-residence at Bristol University, but the English Stage Company persuaded the Arts Council to continue its support for him at the Royal Court. During his time there he adapted Isaac Babel's *Marya* in 1968, and Chekhov's *Uncle Vanya* (from the translation by Nina Froud) which opened on 24 February 1970, starring Paul Scofield in what Martin Esslin called 'the production of a generation'. Hampton's last play as Resident Dramatist, *The Philanthropist*, opened at the Royal Court in July 1970.

Christopher Hampton was only one of the writers to develop in the 'Sunday Night' productions during that year, 1966–7. Peter Gill, whose first play, *The Sleepers Den*, had first been staged in a 'Sunday Night' production in 1964, had a new play, *A Provincial Life* – based on the diaries of Chekhov – produced on 30 October 1966. Perhaps more important, Peter Gill was able to develop as a director during that time and achieved fame for his production of *The Daughter-in-Law*, for which he received the 1968 *Plays and Players* award for the best production of the year, and from 29 February to May 1968, the three Lawrence plays were produced in repertory. At the age of thirty, Peter Gill, almost wholly a product of the Royal Court, had achieved international fame as a director, directing on Broadway and at Stratford, Ontario, as well as in London.

Also during that 1966–7 period, three plays – Joe Orton's *The Ruffian on the Stair*, James Casey's *A View to the Common*, and Michael Rosen's *Backbone* – were given Sunday Night productions and later put into the main bill of the Royal Court.

David Storey is another writer who began work at the Court in 1967 when *The Restoration of Arnold Middleton* was produced. Originally scheduled for a run of two weeks, it proved so popular that it was held over for a third week before being transferred into the West End. Since then, Storey has become a Royal Court 'house writer' and has had six more highly successful plays produced there.

One extremely important advance at the Court began with a series of experimental, low-budget productions in the club-rehearsal room over the main theatre. The club room had been operated by various managements since the founding of the Company. Clement Freud had used the room as a private club when the theatre was being operated by Alfred Esdaile, and, at the Company's insistence, opened the membership to include the members of the English Stage Society. The club had been very important because, besides providing amenities for the Society members, it had provided approximately £2,000 a year income for the Company. By the spring of 1968, however, after the club had operated for a year with only moderate success by the Society itself, Gaskill suggested to the Management Committee that it would be interesting to present a series of experimental productions in order to discover whether the space would work as a studio theatre. With the help of a £500 gift from Lord Sainsbury, fourteen productions – some plays, some mime, some created during rehearsals from a basic idea – were presented during the spring and summer of 1968.

The success of those informal presentations led Gaskill to request that the club room be made into a more fully equipped studio theatre.

The difficulty in making the Theatre Upstairs into a proper public theatre consisted largely in the Greater London Council's insistence on rather crippling fire regulations (such as new exits and fire escapes) – which would have proven very expensive to satisfy. In December 1968, the Arts Council was asked to provide a capital grant of £5,000 to carry out the work, which had already been started under a £4,000 interest-free loan from the English Stage Society. N. V. Linklater, representing the Arts Council, emphasized that it would be necessary to present the work of the new Theatre Upstairs in such a way that it would in no sense compromise or dilute the quality of the main bill work, and also to show the Arts Council that the Theatre Upstairs would not simply be doubling up on the sort of work done by theatres such as the Hampstead Theatre Club and the Open Space Theatre, which were also receiving Arts Council support. Gaskill explained that there was a mass of young directors, writers, and actors to be discovered and that their work could be shown more cheaply and at a faster rate in the studio theatre. He also felt that it would be valuable to have the second theatre because then the Court would be in the privileged position of being able to form a bridge between traditional and experimental theatres. He felt confident that the work of the Theatre Upstairs could only complement and strengthen the work of the main theatre and never dilute it.

The Arts Council's response to the grant application was to alter the balance of subsidy and guarantee against loss so that the Royal Court received £5,000 more in straight subsidy and £5,000 less in guarantee against loss. The most the Company could receive from the Arts Council during the year remained unchanged at £94,000.

Although the Management Committee and Gaskill remained ultimately responsible for budgeting and policy, in all other ways the organization of the Theatre Upstairs was and is self-contained. Nicholas Wright, an assistant director with the Court, was appointed Director of the Theatre Upstairs and, with consultations with the other directors, ran the studio as a separate theatre, making all the day-to-day decisions and the majority of the artistic decisions.

During its first eighteen months of operation, the Theatre Upstairs presented twenty productions, each playing for from one week to ten days. The range of work done has run from the poetic naturalism of Gill's *The Sleepers Den* and *Over Gardens Out* to the wordless *The Pit* – a production created by Peter Dockley which included wrestlers, monsters, and steam – to the traditional *Evening of Music Hall* directed by Roger Croucher. But, in general, the word is still the important thing. Even with Howard Benton's *Revenge*, which was devised and developed in conjunction with the director, Chris Parr, and the actors, the public was finally presented with a polished play for which the author took credit and responsibility.

The plays, when they are fully written scripts, are selected from the general stock which is received at the Court. The directors come either from people working at the Court or from people whose work has been seen outside and who have been invited to do a production at the Theatre Upstairs. In the case of *Beckett 3*, produced in April 1970, Gaskill directed two of them (Roger Croucher directed the third) because he *wanted* to do them and because he thought (rightly) that the public wanted to see them.

The Theatre Upstairs is an open room and, hence, allows great flexibility, both in staging and in the arrangement of seating. The most extreme example of that flexibility was seen in the production of *The Pit*. A scaffolding was erected creating a large pit in which most of the action took place, with the audience – limited to forty – seated or standing around the edge. Just before the end of the performance (it could not properly be called a play) the actors and the audience exchanged areas – the audience was led into the pit and the action continued on the former seating area.

The lack of extensive seating area creates another benefit – less tangible, but nonetheless important: there can be no commercial considerations. Although the productions usually play to full houses, there can never be any question of taking in enough money even to cover expenses: the most that can be seated for any performance is one hundred, although sixty is the more usual number. The criterion is therefore purely artistic. The directors and playwrights have tremendous freedom – freedom that they wouldn't get working even downstairs at the Court. Beyond the usual budget, the artists just don't ever have to think about the commercial aspects of theatre and that freedom allows experimentation which, hopefully, will later influence the broader-based commercial theatre. And the Theatre Upstairs allows that experimentation to be done much more cheaply than in a big theatre. The budget for the first thirteen weeks called for a loss of £5,300, and the actual loss was only £5,249.

Despite the fact that the Theatre Upstairs is operated on a very small budget, has no workshop, no wardrobe, no storage space, and no stage crew, the work done is usually first-rate. The actors, of course, are professional, and rehearsals usually last eight hours a day for three weeks. The décor, though necessarily simple, is never shoddy. The Royal Court's policy of presenting only highly polished productions extends to the Theatre Upstairs.

The writers are paid £50 against ten per cent of the gross takings and, in the case of a new play, the Theatre Upstairs applies to the Arts Council for a grant of £150, which is paid directly to the author. Although the playwrights do rewrite to some extent during rehearsals, nothing – except the multiple-authored *Enoch Show* and *Layby* – has ever been rewritten extensively and it is extremely rare for any rewriting to be done after a show has opened.

Part of the Theatre Upstairs's policy has been to bring in other experimental groups. Under that policy, Upstairs has been host to the Traverse Theatre (Edinburgh) production of Stanely Eveling's *Dear Janet Rosenberg, Dear Mr Kooning*; the Paperbag Players from the U.S.A.; *Raw,* a production devised by the students of Rolle College, Exmouth; the travelling Incubus Theatre Company's production of *An Account of the Marriage of August Strindberg and Harriet Bosse*; and the Experimental Unit of the Royal College of Art and Goldsmiths' College's *Mixed Media Event*.

The Theatre Upstairs has been a continuing success and has seen that success spread beyond its walls – a development which will be dealt with in the next chapter.

The extent to which the English Stage Company will go in support of a play which it finds artistically valuable, but not commercially viable, was demonstrated with the 1969 production of *Life Price*, written by Jeremy Seabrook and Michael O'Neill, both teachers and sociologists. A clinical study of the effects of a child-murder on a community and family, the play received generally good reviews, even though the critics were disturbed by its cold, documentary style. The critics' descriptions of the story, however, did not appeal to the prospective audience and for the first eleven performances, *Life Price* played to only fourteen per cent of box office capacity. Gaskill believed that both the play and the production were valuable, however, and the Management Committee agreed with him. It was decided that, rather than close the play, the Court would give free tickets for the remaining two weeks of the scheduled run. Gaskill said he would never have made such a decision in the case of a real failure, but that *Life Price* had been received with respect and it was 'an example of a play which had no place in the commercial set-up – using that phrase in its largest sense.' The Arts Council gave its permission for the experiment, saying that the Royal Court was free to make its own decisions in such a case and that the subsidy would not be affected. The public response was immediate: all the tickets were taken within the first few days.

Although Gaskill continued to feel that the giving of free seats, at least for one or two productions a year, would be the best way of reaching beyond the fashionable minority to a larger and more varied audience, the costs involved proved far too great for any regular system of free seats to be established.

In 1966 a new Schools' Scheme was introduced, financed by a £5,000 grant from the Arts Council. Under the direction of Jane Howell, an assistant director at the Court, a scheme of afternoon performances and discussions for the schools was put into effect. *Roots* was the first play chosen under the scheme, and the next production, Brendan Behan's *The Hostage*, was performed exclusively for schools and played for matinées during the run of *Three Sisters* in April and May 1967.

The student card scheme, introduced with the production of *Roots*, proved an unqualified success. In the first two years of its operation over 11,000 students attended under the scheme – a figure that does not include the special productions just for schools. During the presentation of *Look Back in Anger* in the autumn of 1968 – presented in the main bill for the public, but with the Schools Scheme in mind – over one hundred students attended every night, and the matinées were entirely composed of students.

One of the most interesting experiments provided by the Schools Scheme was the production of *Revolution* during the summer of 1969 as part of the developing policy of creating projects in which the students themselves could participate and contribute instead of passively watching finished productions. In May, Jane Howell wrote to the 2,500 London schools setting out a proposal for an 'act-in' on the theme of revolution, to culminate in a performance at the Royal Court. Seventeen schools expressed interest and eleven finally provided a total of 140 students to participate in the two-weeks' project. In July the students arrived and 'rehearsals' started. 'Rehearsals' included a trip to a Biafra exhibition, to Harrods, to the National Gallery, to watch the arrival of the Finnish Prime Minister. The students were given talks by speakers from the Squatters' Association, from the London School of Economics, from the Schools Action Committee, by a drug expert, and by others who might answer their questions. After their discussions and visits, the students were told to act out their own reactions and their own problems. During the 'rehearsal' period a gradual balance and pattern emerged and a three-hour performance was developed in which the students acted out their views on school, on colour prejudice, on the false 'permissive society' – which they felt existed only in the eyes of the mass media – and on their fears and hopes as they approached adult life and responsibilities.

Although the final product didn't interest many critics to any great extent, it did provide a great breakthrough in communication with the students and provided them with a novel experience in participatory theatre; and, as Michael Billington said in *The Times*, 'So much secondhand nonsense is written about the younger generation that it is refreshing to have a report direct from the front line.' *Revolution* was so well attended and the audiences responded so well that the large Round House Theatre was taken and the production was presented there for three more performances in August 1969.

Some rehearsals of regular main bill productions are open for students, depending on the director, the actors, and the material. Rehearsals for the 1969 Christmas show, *The Three Musketeers Ride Again*, were always attended by students. The modern pantomime, by and featuring the Alberts, a mad-cap comedy team (creators of *An Evening of British Rubbish*) allowed for, and was probably improved by, the exchange between the performers and the students watching rehearsals – and the Alberts loved working with children. *Uncle Vanya*, on the other hand, could not have been produced with schoolchildren attending rehearsals, but a special production based on the life and writings of Chekhov was presented by a small group of actors for an audience of students and was followed by a lively discussion.

The Royal Court has continued its School Scheme with other productions for schoolchildren, including *Skyvers* by Barry Reckord, which transferred to the Round House, and *Brussels*, written and directed by Jonathan Hales, which transferred to Greenwich. Other productions, such as Paul Foster's *Elizabeth I* in November 1973, have toured the schools after their runs at the Court. Workshops in theatre are also held every Wednesday at Oval House for children aged fifteen and older and in May 1973, the Court held the first of its Young Playwrights Competitions.

Continued support from the Arts Council and, now, from the Inner London Education Authority, has enabled the Royal Court to take positive steps towards educating the young audience in theatre. While hardly alone in its work with schools, the Court's schemes have proved popular and successful and have provided an example of what can be done and how very much more needs to be done in work with youth in drama and theatre.

George Devine, on invitation, had travelled as far abroad as Japan and Brazil to speak about the English Stage Company. Certainly the Royal Court had achieved international fame long before the summer of 1968 when the Company, sponsored by the British Council, took *The Daughter-in-Law* to the Belgrade Festival, where it was awarded first prize as the best production in the Festival. From Belgrade the Company toured to Milan and Venice. Again, in August and September 1969, the British Council sponsored the Company's productions of *Saved* and *Narrow Road to the Deep North* in a more extensive tour: Belgrade, Prague, Warsaw, Dublin, and Venice. *Saved*, damned by the critics and banned by the censor in 1966, was awarded joint first prize in the Belgrade Festival in 1969. Peter Gill again represented the English Stage Company in 1973 when his production of *The Merry Go-Round*, by D. H. Lawrence, played for a week in Brussels as part of the Europalia '73 festival.

In August 1969, at the suggestion of William Gaskill, it was decided to ask Lindsay Anderson and Anthony Page to return to the Royal Court as Associate Artistic Directors. Gaskill felt that he needed a change and that the Court could also do with an infusion of fresh ideas. The Management Committee agreed that all three could operate as Co-Artistic Directors, which would allow them to stay fresh by giving them the freedom to accept outside assignments from time to time. The Company policy remained unchanged – the production of new plays with an occasional revival – and the rest of the 1969–70 season was planned by the Co-Artistic Directors.

Shortly after the announcement of the change in artistic direction, the battle with the critics flared up anew. In a press release, dated 2 October 1969, the Royal Court announced that it would no longer send free tickets to Hilary Spurling, theatre critic for the weekly *Spectator*. The Court explained its position:

> 'There is no question of our barring Mrs Spurling: we are simply not inviting her to review our work. We do not find Mrs Spurling's attitude to our work illuminating, and we do not believe that it furthers our relationship with the public.'

Some of the critics – those from *The Sunday Times*, the *Daily Express*, and the *Evening Standard* – retaliated by boycotting the Court's productions. The press accused Lindsay Anderson (the whole affair was attributed to him although the decision had been made by the three Co-Artistic Directors with the backing of the Management Committee) of censorship, of attacking the very freedom of expression he claimed to champion, and of being bitter about Hilary Spurling's past uncomplimentary reviews of his work. Anderson claimed that those were not at all his reasons. He said, in a private interview:

> 'I'm not against the critics. What I say about the critics is that they, in fact, consciously or unconsciously – and very often unconsciously – stand for a conception of the theatre which limits the theatre's audience. They are naïve when they think that what we want are good notices. The very kind of good notice that they give us is itself damaging. Implicit in the way they write, even im-

plicit in the way they praise, is often a conception of the theatre as a limited middle-class diversion. This is impossible for them to understand because they can only see criticism of them like the one I made in terms of a threat to their jobs . . .

'The one thing I have been told by everbody, including the Arts Council, is that the only basic reason why we cannot withdraw invitations from the *Spectator* is because we have always given them.

'The idea of a radical questioning of anything is abhorrent to the English. This gives them a certain stability and, undoubtedly, from a certain point of view, this is quite a good thing. But from another point of view, it is absolute death.

'And that's one of the reasons I've been so bloody-minded about the whole thing and still am.'

The English Stage Company had seen many of its plays attacked by the critics and had good reason to feel that the critics had done nothing to further the development of drama. The conservative and sometimes fatuous critical attitude which the people at the Court find so ruinous to innovation was precisely pointed out by Martin Esslin – a critic himself – when writing about the struggle to establish Brecht in England:

'Furthermore (and this is a measure of the English critics' inability to contribute to the artistic progress of the English stage) this undeniable influence of "Brechtian" ideas established itself in the face of stubborn and often vicious attacks on Brecht by the vast majority of daily and weekly reviewers, who not only dismissed a whole series of productions of Brecht's plays in English with contempt (which most of them fully deserved) but consistently denounced Brecht himself as a fraud and the inflated idol of faddists and perverse intellectuals.'[3]

George Devine and William Gaskill had been in the forefront of the 'perverse intellectuals' championing Brecht in England, and Esslin's indictment could be applied with equal truth to the critics' reactions to the works of John Arden, Samuel Beckett, Eugene Ionesco, Edward Bond, and many of the other Court writers who broke away from the accepted pattern of what makes a 'good' play.

Nevertheless, the Arts Council felt very strongly its principle that public support of theatre carries with it the necessity of public scrutiny in the form of critical evaluation by the reviewers of the national daily and weekly periodicals; and, after compromise between the warring parties proved impossible, the Arts Council applied its power. In April 1970, the Arts Council threatened to withhold the Royal Court's grant, a week before it was due to be paid, if the Court refused to restore the invitations to the *Spectator*. The Court had no choice but to accede, but fired a final round as it did so, saying, in a press release:

'After all, the privilege of not inviting the *Spectator* was not worth the closure of the theatre. Once again the tanks have rolled and

principle has had to give way to force. The principle we tried to
establish was that theatre critics who accept invitation to review
plays have responsibilities and duties and that the theatre should
have the right to withhold free seats from critics, though never bar
them, just as the critics have the right to refuse invitations.

'The *Spectator* is not an important periodical but we thought,
and still think, that the principle is important.'

Although the Royal Court looks upon the Arts Council's use of its
financial power as a dangerous precedent, the Arts Council felt that
it, too, must act according to its principles and it was therefore un-
willing to change its interpretation of the application of those
principles.

It should be pointed out that the critics themselves are not
oblivious to the shortcomings of the first night reviews and many
have spoken on the subject. Clive Barnes of the *New York Times*,
who is in the often unenviable position of wielding enormous power
over the fate of a production, has even suggested an end to first nights
for the critics, calling for press nights during the previews – thus
reducing the pressure on the performers and allowing the critics to
see the show more than once, if they choose, before publishing their
reviews at the traditional time.

The English Stage Company continued its championing of new
writers and again served as a 'post-graduate course' for star actors
when, on 17 June 1970, David Storey's play, *Home* – his third in little
over a year – opened at the Royal Court starring Sir John Gielgud
and Sir Ralph Richardson, both appearing at the Court for the first
time. Gielgud had said as early as 1956 that he wanted to work with
the English Stage Company, but had never carried out that promise.

The success of *Home* firmly established David Storey as a Royal
Court writer of importance. It met with success not only at the
Court, but also in the West End and in New York where it won the
Drama Critics Circle Award as Best Play of the Year; and it was
made into a television play and shown both in Britain and America,
thus reaching an enormously large audience.

Christopher Hampton's play *The Philanthropist* opened in the
main bill at the Court on 3 August 1970. Although the Court had
thought it a good play, no one expected the smash success that it was
to become. Although the Royal Court has sometimes been accused of
being nothing more than a glorified try-out theatre for plays destined
for the West End, *The Philanthropist* certainly is a case in point of
how silly that contention can be. Hampton's play was accepted for
production while he was still Playwright in Residence at the Court.
Although nothing stipulates that the Company will produce any play
by its resident dramatist, it is always hoped that it will be possible to
produce at least one. *The Philanthropist* was given the normal run
under those circumstances of four weeks. It proved a great success at
the Court and was then transferred to the Mayfair and ran in the
West End for over three years. Certainly, had the Court's prime
motive been to find a success it would have greatly extended the run
in its own theatre and sat back to exploit the play for profit and glory.
But that was not at all the case. On 14 September, *Cancer*, a play by

the young relatively unknown American playwright Michael Weller, opened as scheduled.

The day after the opening of *The Philanthropist*, 4 August 1970, Neville Blond died. He had had a long, successful, and remarkably diverse career. A man of great and restless energy, at the age of fifty-nine he had undertaken a project in a field about which he knew very little – the theatre. The English Stage Company was known in the Blond family as 'Neville's Folly'. But Neville Blond was not a dilet-tante – he approached the fledgling English Stage Company with the same astuteness, business acumen, and wit that he brought to his many other ventures. Nor did he desert the Company when the going got rough or when he did not agree with the production of any par-ticular play. He oversaw the business end of the Company with remarkable attention to detail – chairing bi-weekly Management Committee meetings from the beginning until two weeks before his death. Even in the last days of his illness he was very, very tough. His control of the financial side of the Company was masterly. He did not condemn failure, but he fought to find successes to balance the finan-cial failures in order to keep the Company going. Both Devine and Gaskill often had to fight with him, but something in those battles provided a good working relationship. They knew that he cared about the money and about the continuation of the Company, and that was his strength. There is absolutely no doubt that without that care and personal support in the form of contributions and loan guarantees, the English Stage Company could not have survived.

In his resignation speech, George Devine put it this way:

'You all realize what an enterprise of this kind owes to its Chair-man. Since the English Stage Company has become international-ly well-known I have had many visitors asking me the secret of founding such an enterprise. My answer has always been the same – "Find yourself a good Chairman." Well, we were lucky – we have found one and you all know his name ... I commend to you a man who will foster his "folly" to the utmost of his strength, through thick and thin, and emerge a punchdrunk but undaunted lion.'

George Devine may have been the soul of the English Stage Com-pany, but for fifteen years Neville Blond was its life-giving heart.

The English Stage Company entered its fifteenth year of operation with past successes internationally recognized and its original policy of promoting new talent and particularly new writing talent still in effect. William Gaskill, Lindsay Anderson, and Anthony Page con-tinued the artistic direction, but the death of Neville Blond necessitated changes in management and two years later the artistic direction also changed.

## Notes

1. The Willett Report was the result of a two-year study launched by the Drama Panel in 1964 at the Arts Council's request and sub-mitted to the Council in January 1967.

2. 'Sir Alec in Interview,' *Daily Express*, 22 October 1966.
3. Martin Esslin, *Reflections: Essays on Modern Theatre*, Doubleday and Company, Inc., New York, 1969, pp. 75–6.

# 6 Present Policy, future Hopes

Greville Poke was asked by the Council of the English Stage Company to become the new Chairman. He had served as Honorary Secretary from the beginning and in that capacity had worked closely with Neville Blond throughout the years. However, there had been a considerable divergence of view over the Hilary Spurling affair and Poke had been very much against the stand that was taken by the Company. In view of that, he felt that he would not be fully accepted as Chairman at that time and refused the position, although he continued to serve as Honorary Secretary.

Oscar Lewenstein and Robin Fox agreed to become joint Chairmen. Both had been with the Company from the beginning, both had served as Company Manager, both had remained active on the Management Committee, and both had developed successful careers as respected and imaginative producers away from the Royal Court. After Robin Fox's tragic death on 21 January 1971, Lewenstein assumed sole responsibility as Chairman.

But the changes on the management side of the Company did not interrupt the artistic output. After the run of *Cancer* in September and early October, an exciting and novel festival was held at the Court – *Come Together*.

Early in the year Gaskill had begun a search of 'experimental' or 'exploratory' theatre groups. He wanted to look at a cross-section of their work – which was being performed in club and fringe theatres, at arts centres, and in arts laboratories – and to assess its importance and relevance to the new work of the more traditional 'literary' theatre. The New Activities Committee of the Arts Council had allocated £15,000 to finance gatherings in each of the eight regional divisions, each organized autonomously and each with its own individual character. The main aim was to investigate and promote 'new activities' and each region would show the work of local groups – though, in fact, many London-based groups appeared at several of the gatherings. The object of the *Come Together* festival was to show the best of the regional festivals' work in London at the Royal Court – partly to give the work the recognition it deserves and partly to see it in the context of a writers' theatre in the hope that there might be a cross-fertilization between the different kinds of work shown and thus be a stimulus for future work in the theatre generally.

In order to accommodate the twenty groups who participated in the festival great changes had to be made to the Royal Court Theatre itself. The theatre building is inflexible and cramped and does not lend itself easily to different forms of production. As Gaskill pointed out, it would have been easier to hold the festival in a freer space like

the Round House, but 'in a way this would have been too obvious
a solution.' Therefore it was decided to change the Court itself. The
seats in the stalls were removed, the stage was raised and extended to
form a large projecting apron, and there was a pit or promenade in
which people could sit or walk about – much like the popular
Elizabethan theatre with the yard and the galleries above it. There
was also tiered seating on the stage to allow for the productions in the
round. The Theatre Upstairs was also used, as was Sloane Square
itself and even the phone box in the Underground station. The
festival lasted twenty days with the activities running most days all
day and far into the night. The audience could go to several performances a day for five shillings.

The companies who performed were heterogeneous and the types
of performance diverse. There was the somewhat traditional *The
Whitby Lifeboat Disaster* by Peter Terson from Peter Cheeseman's
Victoria, Stoke-on-Trent; and there was Stuart Brisley's audience
participation show. While eating brown bread and drinking water,
Brisley taunted the audience while his group slowly built a
scaffolding. When the audience called back the cast would repeat
their calls with malice, thus calling fourth new taunts. The climax occurred when Brisley climbed to the top of the scaffolding and
vomited. The Gentle Fire played a John Cage piece and the audience
felt free to add its catcalls and whistles. The CAST Company
screamed its piece through microphones, accompanied by
excruciatingly loud unorchestrated noises and explosions in the
Theatre Upstairs and the show was followed by lively discussions
which also ended in loud sounds from both cast and audience. And
outside or in the lobby or the bars Peter Kuttner served up rainbow
coloured bread and green hamburgers. Peter Dockley staged a kind of
freak show in which the audience was led in small groups into a room
full of blue-painted bodies, chicken feathers, chicken coops, chickens.
Dry-ice steam floated about, chains clanked, sounds screeched, and
the whole thing slowly created a strange sense of ritualistic reality
full of meaning. Ken Campbell's Road Show brought their pub pieces
and sang dirty songs, told very funny stories, changed a boy into a
chicken, and performed a series of sketches taken from modern
folklore or yesterday's newspaper that provided many a good laugh
over rape, madness, mutilation, and perversion. The Theatre
Upstairs presented Heathcote Williams's *AC/DC* and Howard Brenton's *Christie In Love*; and Carlyle Reedy performed a dream-like
ritual with a fish and projections. There were the People Show, The
Freehold, and all around – in the theatre, in the street, in the square –
was pop and folk music.

It would be impossible to assess the extent of cross-fertilization
which the *Come Together* festival may have provided, but there is no
doubt that both audiences and artists were exposed to an exciting
and broad array of the vital streams in and around the English
theatre.

The *Come Together* festival was followed by a three-week run of
Williams's *AC/DC* on the main bill, thus providing the first transfer
of a play from Upstairs to the main stage. Because of the great
differences in the sizes and basic arrangements of the two theatres, it

is very difficult to move a play from the Theatre Upstairs. The main stage of the Court, because of the proscenium and the inflexibility of the seating, demands extensive re-directing and, for many shows, even rewriting. Most of the shows produced Upstairs simply could not maintain their effect in even the medium-sized Royal Court. It is interesting to note the careful, sometimes unusual, choice of theatres for the subsequent transfers from the Theatre Upstairs.

In 1971 E. A. Whitehead's *The Foursome* transferred to the Fortune Theatre, which is a small house about the size of the Royal Court. But even that move necessitated completely re-designing and re-staging the original production. In November 1973, *The Foursome* was produced in New York and, although it was a new production, again a small theatre was chosen.

Also in 1971, Athol Fugard's *Boseman and Lena* was transferred to the Young Vic – which has a highly flexible, intimate theatre.

The most interesting and by far most successful transfer was of the 1973 production of Richard O'Brien's camp rock musical *The Rocky Horror Show*. Played in the Theatre Upstairs in an imaginatively camp cinema setting to an audience of only sixty, the action necessarily flowed on all sides and on a ramp through the centre of the audience. It was imperative to find a theatre that would allow the same eerie intimacy as that achieved Upstairs. Michael White invested in the show and transferred it first to the Chelsea Classic Cinema and later to the Essoldo Cinema, King's Road. It is significant that in both cases the transfer was to an unusual theatre setting and that a great deal of trouble and money was spent on converting the cinemas in order to retain the right environmental aspects of the production. The better a show is suited to Upstairs, the more re-thinking and the more money is necessary for a successful transfer.

Money is still a large factor in the planning of the Theatre Upstairs. The actors and staff – who receive pay of only £18 a week – in effect, subsidize the theatre. The Arts Council still doesn't give the Theatre Upstairs a direct subsidy. The parent English Stage Company allows a portion of its grant for productions Upstairs – £16,000 for the 1973–4 season. In addition, the box office provides approximately £7,000. However, Upstairs still faced a deficit for 1973–4 of about £4,000, thus making the huge success of *The Rocky Horror Show* all the more welcome.

Nevertheless, the non-commercial freedom is still at the heart of the Theatre Upstairs policy. In fact, there have been few changes Upstairs since its inception in 1968. In March 1971, Nicholas Wright resigned as Director and went to Stratford, Ontario as Peter Gill's assistant. Roger Croucher, who had been an assistant at the Court and had worked Upstairs from the first, became the new Director.

During Croucher's period there were some changes made. Originally shows were presented for from one week to ten days with the theatre dark between productions. Runs had been pushed to two weeks when he took over, but he felt that good work was being squandered because so few people were able to see it and so extended the runs to four weeks. That time was also very lucky in relation to the groups that came in – Pip Simmons, The Freehold Company,

Ken Campbell – and in the fact that there happened to be many good scripts to do. During Croucher's direction the Theatre Upstairs also had its first tour – *AC/DC*, which went to Edinburgh's Traverse Theatre, Canterbury, and several other places. That tour was followed later in 1971 by a similar tour of *Corona*, a musical by Keith Dewhurst and Bill Bryden.

In August 1972, Nicholas Wright again assumed the position of Director. Croucher had been at the Court for four years and, after an exhausting eighteen months directing the Theatre Upstairs, felt it was time for a change. People outside the theatre seldom realize how fatiguing it is to attend to the day-to-day details of running a theatre – even a small one – while at the same time overseeing the artistic side of selecting and producing a continuous season of new plays. Both Wright and Croucher had had to perform both jobs.

Under Wright's new régime the policies have remained essentially the same – new plays with runs of four weeks, occasional visiting groups with runs of two weeks, and an intermittent tour. *Sizwe Bansi is Dead*, devised by Athol Fugard, John Kani, and Winston Ntshona and performed Upstairs in September and October, 1973, was set up from its inception to tour and after travelling a circuit which took it from Exeter to Dublin in November and December, returned to play a season in the Royal Court's main bill. When Wright returned to Upstairs the job had become more attractive – a business manager was hired to lighten the load on the Director and new office space (eventually located in Holbein Place, just around the corner from Sloane Square) was promised by Oscar Lewenstein, who had become Artistic Director of the English Stage Company in July 1972, with Greville Poke assuming the position of Chairman.

The decisions of the Co-Artistic Directors – William Gaskill, Lindsay Anderson, and Anthony Page – to resign were personal and varied. Page had always wanted to be a freelance director with a base; he never really wanted to run a theatre in the sense of creating policy or making new plans for development. Anderson, though very good at it, never really liked running the administrative side of a theatre; he had a film he wanted to make (*Oh, Lucky Man!*) and when he makes a film a complete year is absorbed in it during which time he won't do anything else or think of anything else. Gaskill wanted a break from administering, to get away and direct elsewhere without the constant worries of running a theatre. He had begun to take six- or nine-month periods off in 1969, working in rotation with Page and Anderson, but finally felt that that arrangement was not really working out, that some one person has to be in charge, that the Court is a theatre which demands total commitment. Gaskill, Page, and Anderson all have strong personalities, but they had all worked in the Court for many years and were used to each other. But quarrels did arise – usually over the more trivial things which are normally decided upon almost automatically – and they had to be discussed and thrashed out. There was surprisingly close agreement about the choice of any particular play or what was to be done in the next season. And the record of plays done during their period together is very fine indeed. Beginning with Storey's *The Contractor* in October 1969, (when, in fact, Gaskill was on his first leave) and spanning some two years to John Osborne's adaptation of *Hedda Gabler* in June 1972, a wide range of new plays and revivals had been done.

After a great deal of discussion it was decided that Lewenstein should become Artistic Director with overall administrative powers and that Gaskill, Page, and Anderson would remain as associates, still to be very much part of the planning of policy and to direct when they were free to and wanted to. Gaskill finally decided that after having run the theatre for so long he would not be able to exist in that relationship with another Artistic Director. He felt that it would be a good opportunity to make a clean break, knowing that he could always direct there if he wanted.

It is important that the sense of continuity has been maintained at the Court. Oscar Lewenstein was the natural choice to become Artistic Director – he had been a founder of the Company, had worked closely with it ever since, and had been an influential and courageous producer in his own right. He was available, wanted the job, and wanted to keep as many of the previous artistic directors as possible as associates. But Gaskill, among others, feels that it would have been better to have a working artist as Artistic Director and that, perhaps, a break with the past would not be altogether a bad thing.

Yet, Anderson and Page continued to work as Associate Artistic Directors, joined first by Peter Gill and later by Albert Finney, and Gaskill has returned to direct Edward Bond's *The Sea*. The continuity of the writer/director relationships which have developed over the years – and which continue to form among the new generation of writers and directors at the Court – is important.

Early in the history Tony Richardson directed the Osborne plays – *Look Back in Anger, The Entertainer, Luther*. Another early relationship developed between John Dexter and Arnold Wesker. The first Wesker play directed by Dexter was *Chicken Soup with Barley* at the Belgrade Theatre, Coventry, which later came to the Court; then came *Roots, The Kitchen, I'm Talking About Jerusalem, Chips With Everything*, and when Wesker returned to the Royal Court with *The Old Ones* in August 1972, Dexter again directed even though he hadn't worked at the Court in over nine years. Dexter did not direct Wesker's *Their Very Own and Golden City* (Gaskill did) because he didn't like the play – and directors do not direct out of friendship but out of love for the play. That, of course, is essential in all the writer/director relationships. The most consistent and longest lasting of these relationships have been between Bond and Gaskill and Storey and Anderson. Although Keith Johnstone directed Bond's first play, *The Pope's Wedding*, it was Gaskill's sympathy with and championing of his work which allowed much of it to be produced at all and Gaskill has continued directing Bond's plays, including *Lear* in 1971 and *The Sea* in 1973. Beginning with the film version of *This Sporting Life*, Anderson has directed all of the Storey plays, with the exception of *The Restoration of Arnold Middleton*, directed by Robert Kidd, and *Cromwell*, which was directed by Anthony Page in August 1973 – just prior to Anderson's production of *The Farm* in September 1973. The same sort of relationship has developed between Robert Kidd and Christopher

Hampton – Kidd has directed all of Hampton's plays from *When Did You Last See My Mother* in 1966 through to the 1973 production of *Savages*, with the exception of Hampton's adaptation of *Uncle Vanya*. A more recent writer/director relationship at the Court has developed between Howard Brenton and Max Stafford-Clark, who has directed three Brenton plays – *Christie In Love* and *Hitler Dances* Upstairs and the June 1973 production, *Magnificence*, in the main theatre. The relationships tend to develop because of a mutual respect between the artists involved and the growth of a working understanding. Then, too, none of the directors has cut himself off from the work of other writers and if the sympathy should dissolve the writers can always go to different directors.

The Royal Court has been accused of living off the past, of having developed successful playwrights who have become commercial or popular and then producing their plays again and again, that it has become a tryout theatre for its own house writers – while ignoring its real objective, the fostering of new, undeveloped playwrights. At a glance that may appear true, but on further study the argument becomes insubstantial. The playwrights in question – Osborne, Bond, Hampton, Storey – have certainly had a number of productions at the Court from 1970 through 1973: Osborne two plus one adaptation, Bond two, Hampton two plus one adaptation, and Storey four. It is easy to say that a play should have been produced in the commercial theatre once that play has been a success, but until that play is in fact a success it is not always possible to find a commercial producer.

Certainly Edward Bond, after having six plays produced at the Royal Court over an eleven-year period, would not readily find a commercial producer in the West End – although he is a much-produced star playwright in Germany. *Lear*, Bond's monumental, unrelentingly gloomy masterpiece, could never have found commercial production in England. It played to only twenty-eight per cent of seating capacity at the Royal Court. Even *The Sea*, which is by far his most accessible play, full of humour and relatively mellow in outlook (especially when compared to *Lear*), did not play to full houses in spite of the presence of Ian Holm and Coral Browne in the cast. Without the continued support of the Royal Court there is absolutely no doubt that Bond – one of the most brilliant playwrights writing today – would have long ago been lost to the theatre.

Christopher Hampton has had four plays and two adaptations produced at the Court over a seven-year period. *The Philanthropist* was his first big success. It is a small, brilliantly witty play written in more or less realistic form – although an onstage suicide near the opening in which an exasperated playwright blows his brains all over the back wall is made the more surprising because of the hilarity with which it is treated. Hampton's next play, *Savages*, however, was not traditional in form. A combination of studies – one a witty study of the kidnapping, self-recognition, and murder of a British diplomat; the other a semi-documentary about the brutal extermination of Brazilian Indians – the play combines flashbacks, present realism, Indian ritual, and quitely spoken accounts of their life and culture. Although the play sometimes sinks under the weight of its theme and the sometimes heavy-handedness of its satire, it does mark a definite advance for Hampton and one which certainly carried high commercial risk.

David Storey's career at the Royal Court has been extraordinary. From his first Royal Court production, *The Restoration of Arnold Middleton* in July 1967 (first produced at the Traverse Theatre, Edinburgh) through to *The Farm* in September 1973, Storey had seven plays produced at the Court and it has been argued that he should no longer submit his plays there but rather take them directly to the West End. After all, since *The Restoration of Arnold Middleton*, three other Storey plays had transferred to commercial theatres – *The Contractor* and *Home* in 1970, and *The Changing Room* in 1972 – and all three had also been produced commercially in New York. But, odd as it seems, Storey would still have trouble finding a commercial producer. There are identifiable characteristics to his plays – slight plots, a poetic circular motion of structure, life seen as a constant battle – but the plays are certainly not predictable. The Royal Court has provided a place for this remarkable playwright to experiment and grow. The 1973 *Cromwell* was written in blank verse. Although not a complete artistic success, no-one would argue that it should not have been done, that Storey should stick to writing the sort of play he has proved himself able to write. *Cromwell* is an adventurous play and even those who did not like it appreciated that here was a major talent stretching himself still further.

Surprisingly even John Osborne still needs the Court. Certainly *A Sense of Detachment* (1972) was not commercial and yet it represented a new form for Osborne. Many of the recognizably Osborne traits are there – the pre-emptive strike, the wit, the xenophobia, the despair for dying excellence – but the form has changed to reflect Osborne's thesis of the dissolution of quality. Should Osborne be told that he could easily rewrite the play into a more acceptable form and then, with his long list of past successes to support him, find a commercial producer? Obviously not. *A Sense of Detachment* represents a reaching out, a development of talent and may represent a seminal point in Osborne's career.

The directors of the Royal Court choose plays because they believe them to be good. A play would not be chosen that had no merit other than that it might run for a long time. But if a play is serious and the only reason for rejecting it was because it might also be successful, it would be madness to turn it away. (It would also mean that the Company would be bankrupt very quickly, for the successes still support the financial failures.) It is important that the Royal Court 'house writers' be allowed to continue their growth and experimentation. But it is also important that young, less established writers be encouraged. That is partly accomplished at the Theatre Upstairs, but that, of course, is not the answer. The fact remains that, after eighteen years, the Royal Court is still the only major space – in terms not only of size but also in terms of the public eye – that developing writers can use or try to get into.

Part of the answer to supporting new writing talent has come in the form of the Resident Dramatist programme, with Christopher Hampton the first to fill that position in 1968–9. The Resident

Dramatist is selected by the Artistic Committee. Basically they try to choose one who has established his seriousness and who might benefit by having the position. They want to do something which will benefit the playwright rather than the Court, although if it does one it will very likely do the other. But each playwright – because of the different personalities – has played a different part in the life of the Court during his period of residency.

The position carries no specific requirements. Hampton became head of the script department, reading and evaluating plays received at the Court; but, more important, he also watched the directors at work and received a practical education. David Hare had already spent a time reading plays at the Court when he became Resident Dramatist in 1970–71 and had become a playwright partly in reaction to that experience. E. A. Whitehead had already had *The Four-some* produced at the Theatre Upstairs when he became Resident Dramatist in 1971. He used his residence there to buy time to think and to work. He hardly ever appeared at the Court, but there were no complaints and he turned in a major script. Howard Brenton, who, like David Hare, came out of Cambridge and then the fringe theatre and small touring companies, wanted to study the operation of a larger theatre. He wants to be a public dramatist and that means understanding the workings of a larger space and even how to run a large theatre – although he also reads scripts which have been sent in. How Michael Abbensetts, who became Resident Dramatist in the autumn of 1973, uses his time remains to be seen. The point is that *how* a Resident Dramatist uses his time is entirely up to him; no one requires him to do anything.

Each Resident Dramatist has had at least one play produced while he was at the Court. Besides Hampton's plays, the Court produced Hare's *Slag* in March 1971; Whitehead's *Alpha Beta* in January 1972 (*Alpha Beta* then transferred to the Apollo Theatre and was produced in New York in 1973); and Howard Brenton's *Magnificence* in 1973.

But the Court has encouraged the coming playwrights with more than the Resident Dramatist programme and Howard Brenton is a case in point. One of Brenton's first plays, *It's My Criminal* was produced as a 'Sunday Night' production in August 1966, and was greeted with howls of derision. Brenton had given up his job working in a restaurant on the South Coast to be involved with the production and found himself stuck in London without job or money. The Court gave him a job as a stagehand and then Gaskill helped find him another job. During that time he wrote *Revenge*, which was produced by the Theatre Upstairs in September 1969, and on the strength of that he got an Arts Council grant. He and a group of other young artists – including David Hare – formed a group called the Portable Theatre and Brenton continued to write for them and for the Traverse Theatre Workshop, and during that period the Theatre Upstairs also did two more Brenton plays – *Christie In Love* and *Hitler Dances*. It was in that period also that Gaskill commissioned plays from twelve writers and *Magnificence* was one of them.

Although the commission carries a payment of only £100 and another £100 on account against royalties if it is accepted, it actually means much more than that. It gives focus and energy to the work in that the playwright knows the space it is being written for and to whom he is going to deliver it. And the Court has accepted most of the plays that were commissioned, for production either in the main bill or Upstairs.

Brenton also feels that it took a great deal of courage for the Court to put on *Magnificence* at all. His plays had created a great deal of trouble and outrage at other theatres: *Christie In Love* had been attacked and nearly prosecuted for obscenity in Brighton and his version of *Measure for Measure* had had similar problems in Exeter while Brenton was Resident Dramatist at the Royal Court. So, as Brenton put it, 'It shows some courage in what is said to be an orthodox and middle-aged and safe theatre to appoint me, first, and to put my play on.' And in order to fit *Magnificence*, and another new play, *The Removalists*, by the young Australian playwright David Williamson, into the schedule it was necessary to set back the production of Storey's *Cromwell* seven weeks – and *Cromwell* had been waiting about eighteen months for a production as it was.

The Royal Court is crowded now. In the autumn of 1970 there were very few worthwhile new plays to be done. About a year later there was a sudden flood of good new plays and it continued into 1974 – and the plays have come from both generations at the Court.

The Royal Court has also been attacked on the grounds that star actors support the work of new writers. It is true – star actors *do* support the work of new writers at the Court; but that would seem to be grounds for praise of both the stars and the theatre. Actors still receive only £30–£50 a week while working at the Court – stars included. The fact is, the Royal Court has a prestige earned through consistently excellent standards and is still the most interesting place to work. Even if the play proves a failure, the rehearsals are great. It *is* a damning fact that audiences still respond more to a star name than to the chance to see key work which may not have a star appearing in it. Ann Jellicoe's *The Sport of My Mad Mother*, one of the real seminal plays, once had an audience of two (under Equity rules the play cannot be performed when the number of people in the audience is fewer than the number of people in the cast; but in true Court tradition, they played it nonetheless); John Antrobus's *Crete and Sergeant Pepper* received excellent reviews and yet could not attract an audience; *Magnificence*, which received notices roughly similar to those of *Savages* but which did not have a star name in the cast, played to very small houses. The problem of depending on star actors to foster recognition and success for new writers has been with the Court from the beginning and it is very likely to remain a problem.

The Royal Court, from its inception, meant to popularize good, meaningful theatre. They *should* transfer plays; they should flood the West End with plays that they believe in. But the Royal Court must also continue to attract new talent; if it doesn't, it will die. It must constantly renew itself with a new generation of Hamptons, of Brentons, of Hares, of Whiteheads, of Abbensetts and it must begin to develop a generation which is younger still.

If the English Stage Company is to continue to exist as a live entity and not merely survive as an ossified institution with a great history, it must maintain the flexibility to reach out for the new, always to be ahead of its time.

# Appendix A
# List of Plays

| Date | Play | Author | Director |
|------|------|--------|----------|
| **1956** | | | |
| 2 April | *The Mulberry Bush* | Angus Wilson | George Devine |
| 9 April | *The Crucible* | Arthur Miller | George Devine |
| 8 May | *Look Back in Anger* | John Osborne | Tony Richardson |
| 15 May | *Don Juan* and *The Death of Satan* | Ronald Duncan | George Devine |
| 26 June | *Cards of Identity* | Nigel Dennis | Tony Richardson |
| 31 Oct | *The Good Woman of Setzuan* | Bertolt Brecht Trans: Eric Bentley | George Devine |
| 12 Dec | *The Country Wife* | William Wycherley | George Devine |
| **1957** | | | |
| 5 Feb | *Member of the Wedding* | Carson McCullers | Tony Richardson |
| 3 April | *Fin de Partie* and *Acte Sans Parole* | Samuel Beckett | Roger Blin Deryk Mendel |
| 10 April | *The Entertainer* | John Osborne | Tony Richardson |
| 14 May | *The Apollo de Bellac* | Jean Giraudoux Adapt: Ronald Duncan | Tony Richardson |
| 14 May | *The Chairs* | Eugène Ionesco Trans: Donald Watson | Tony Richardson |
| 26 May | *The Correspondence Course*● | Charles Robinson | Peter Coe |
| 9 June | *Yes—And After*● | Michael Hastings | John Dexter |
| 25 June | *The Making of Moo* | Nigel Dennis | Tony Richardson |
| 30 June | *The Waiting of Lester Abbs*● | Kathleen Sully | Lindsay Anderson |
| 22 July | *Purgatory* (Devon Festival) | W. B. Yeats | John Dexter |
| 5 Aug | *How Can We Save Father* | Oliver M. Wilkinson | Peter Wood |
| 17 Sep | *Nekrassov* | Jean-Paul Sartre Trans: Sylvia and George Lesson | George Devine |
| 20 Oct | *The Waters Of Babylon*● | John Arden | Graham Evans |
| 26 Nov | *Requiem for a Nun* | William Faulkner | Tony Richardson |
| 1 Dec | *A Resounding Tinkle*● | N. F. Simpson | William Gaskill |
| 26 Dec | *Lysistrata* | Aristophanes Adapt: Dudley Fitts | Minos Volonakis |
| **1958** | | | |
| 11 Feb | *Epitaph for George Dillon* | John Osborne and Anthony Creighton | William Gaskill |

● 'Sunday Night' productions.

| Date | Play | Author | Director |
|------|------|--------|----------|
| **1958** | | | |
| 16 Feb | *Love From Margaret** | Evelyn Ford | John Wood |
| 25 Feb | *The Sport of My Mad Mother* | Ann Jellicoe | George Devine<br>Ann Jellicoe |
| 9 Mar | *The Tenth Chance** | Stuart Holroyd | Anthony Creighton |
| 23 Mar | *Each His Own Wilderness* | Doris Lessing | John Dexter |
| 25 Mar | *The Catalyst* (Arts Theatre) | Ronald Duncan | Phil Brown |
| 2 April | *A Resounding Tinkle* | N. F. Simpson | William Gaskill |
| 2 April | *The Hole* | N. F. Simpson | William Gaskill |
| 21 May | *Flesh to a Tiger* | Barry Reckord | Tony Richardson |
| 18 June | *The Lesson* | Eugène Ionesco | Tony Richardson |
| 22 June | *Brixham Regatta** | Keith Johnstone | William Gaskill |
| 22 June | *For Children** | Keith Johnstone | Ann Jellicoe |
| 7 July | *Gay Landscape*<br>(Citizens Theatre, Glasgow) | George Munro | Peter Duguid |
| 14 July | *Chicken Soup with Barley*<br>(Belgrade Theatre, Coventry) | Arnold Wesker | John Dexter |
| 21 July | *The Private Prosecutor*<br>(Salisbury Arts Theatre) | Thomas Wiseman | Derek Benfield |
| 28 July | *Dear Augustine*<br>(Leatherhead Repertory<br>Theatre) | Alison Macleod | Jordan Lawrence |
| 28 Aug | *Major Barbara* | George Bernard<br>Shaw | George Devine |
| 14 Sep | *Lady On The Barometer** | Donald Howarth | Miriam Brickman<br>Donald Howarth |
| 30 Sep | *Live Like Pigs* | John Arden | George Devine<br>Anthony Page |
| 5 Oct | *Evening of Negro Poetry* | Black and Unknown<br>Bards | Gordon Heath |
| 19 Oct | *Actors Rehearsal Group* | McGrath, Arden,<br>Johnstone,<br>Frank Hatt,<br>Gillian Richards | Anthony Page<br>Miriam Brickman<br>Ann Jellicoe |
| 28 Oct | *End-Game* | Samuel Beckett | George Devine |
| 28 Oct | *Krapp's Last Tape* | Samuel Beckett | Donald McWhinnie |
| 30 Nov | *Displaced Affections** | George Hulme | Phil Brown |
| 4 Dec | *Moon on a Rainbow Shawl* | Errol John | Frith Banbury |
| **1959** | | | |
| 7 Jan | *The Long and the Short and<br>the Tall* | Willis Hall | Lindsay Anderson |
| 8 Feb | *Progress To The Park** | Alun Owen | Lindsay Anderson |
| 15 Mar | *A Resounding Tinkle*<br>(Cambridge A.D.C.) | N. F. Simpson | John Bird |
| 9 April | *Sugar in the Morning* | Donald Howarth | William Gaskill |
| 19 April | *Leonce And Lena** | George Büchner | Michael Geliot |
| 26 April | *Jazzetry** | Christopher Logue | Lindsay Anderson |
| 14 May | *Orpheus Descending* | Tennessee Williams | Tony Richardson |
| 17 May | *The Shameless Professor** | Pirandello | Victor Rietty |
| 30 June | *Roots* | Arnold Wesker | John Dexter |
| 19 July | *Eleven Men Dead at Hola<br>Camp** | Keith Johnstone<br>and<br>William Gaskill | Keith Johnstone<br>and<br>William Gaskill |

\* 'Sunday Night' productions.

| Date | Play | Author | Director |
|---|---|---|---|
| **1959** | | | |
| 29 July | *Look After Lulu* | Noel Coward | Tony Richardson |
| 6 Sept | *The Kitchen* | Arnold Wesker | John Dexter |
| 17 Sept | *Cock-a-Doodle-Dandy* | Sean O'Casey | George Devine |
| 22 Oct | *Serjeant Musgrave's Dance* | John Arden | Lindsay Anderson |
| 1 Nov | *The Invention** | Wole Soyinka | Wole Soyinka |
| 18 Nov | *Rosmersholm* | Henrik Ibsen Trans: Ann Jellicoe | George Devine |
| 22 Nov | *The Naming of Murderers' Rock** | Frederick Bland | John Bird |
| 29 Nov | *Recital* | Ronai Segal | John Bird |
| 22 Dec | *One Way Pendulum* | N. F. Simpson | William Gaskill |
| **1960** | | | |
| 24 Jan | *Christopher Sly** | Thomas Eastwood and Ronald Duncan | Colin Graham |
| 27 Jan | *The Lily White Boys* | Harry Cookson | Lindsay Anderson |
| 8 Mar | *The Room* | Harold Pinter | Anthony Page |
| 8 Mar | *The Dumb Waiter* | Harold Pinter | James Roose-Evans |
| 20 Mar | *One Leg Over The Wrong Wall** | Albert Bermel | John Blatchley |
| 30 Mar | *The Naming of Murderers' Rock* | Frederick Bland | John Bird |
| 10 April | *Eleven Plus** | Kon Fraser | Keith Johnstone |
| 28 April | *Rhinoceros* | Eugène Ionesco Trans: Derek Prouse | Orson Welles |
| 1 May | *The Sport Of My Mad Mother** (Bristol Old Vic Theatre School) | Ann Jellicoe | Jane Howell |
| 27 July | *I'm Talking About Jerusalem* | Arnold Wesker | John Dexter |
| 11 July | *Sea At Dauphin And Six In The Rain** | Derek Walcott | Lloyd Reckord |
| 14 Aug | *The Keep** | Gwyn Thomas | Graham Crowden |
| 14 Sept | *The Happy Haven* | John Arden | William Gaskill |
| 13 Oct | *Platonov* | Chekhov Trans: Dmitri Makaroff | George Devine John Blatchley |
| 23 Oct | *You In Your Small Corner** | Barry Reckord | John Bird |
| 23 Nov | *Trials by Logue* | Christopher Logue | Lindsay Anderson |
| 27 Nov | *The Maimed** | Bartho Smit | Keith Johnstone |
| 11 Dec | *On The Wall** | Henry Chapman | Peter Duguid |
| 18 Dec | *Song In The Theatre** | | Bernard Shaktman |
| 29 Dec | *The Lion in Love* | Shelagh Delaney | Clive Barker |
| **1961** | | | |
| 24 Jan | *The Importance of Being Oscar* | Michael MacLiammoir | Hilton Edwards |
| 21 Feb | *The Changeling* | Middleton and Rowley | Tony Richardson |

* 'Sunday Night' productions.

| Date | Play | Author | Director |
|------|------|--------|----------|
| **1961** | | | |
| 22 Mar | *Jacques* | Eugène Ionesco | R. D. Smith |
| 19 April | *Altona* | Jean-Paul Sartre Adapt: Justin O'Brien | John Berry |
| 7 May | *The Departures** | Jacques Languirand | John Blatchley |
| 28 May | *The Triple Alliance** | J. A. Cuddon | Keith Johnstone |
| 30 May | *The Blacks* | Jean Genet Trans: Bernard Frechtman | Roger Blin |
| 8 June | *Empress With Teapot** | B. R. Whiting | Nicholas Garland |
| 27 June | *The Kitchen* | Arnold Wesker | John Dexter |
| 27 July | *Luther* | John Osborne | Tony Richardson |
| 13 Aug | *Humphrey, Armand and the Artichoke** | G. Roy Levin | Piers Haggard |
| 12 Sept | *August for the People* | Nigel Dennis | George Devine |
| 24 Oct | *The Death of Bessie Smith* and *The American Dream* | Edward Albee | Peter Yates |
| 13 Nov | *That's Us* | Henry Chapman | William Gaskill |
| 22 Nov | *The Keep* | Gwyn Thomas | John Dexter |
| 26 Nov | *Fando And Lis* and *Orison** | Fernando Arrabal Trans: Barbara Wright | Nicholas Garland |
| 3 Dec | *The Scarecrow** | Derek Marlowe | Corin Redgrave |
| 21 Dec | *The Fire Raisers* and *Box and Cox* | Max Frisch Trans: Michael Bullock J. Maddison Morton | Lindsay Anderson |
| **1962** | | | |
| 24 Jan | *A Midsummer Night's Dream* | William Shakespeare | Tony Richardson |
| 28 Jan | *Sacred Cow** | Kon Fraser | Keith Johnstone |
| 18 Feb | *Twelfth Night** | William Shakespeare | George Devine |
| 25 Feb | *The Prisoners* | A dramatic anthology by Tomorrow's Audience | John Duncan |
| 27 Mar | *The Knack* | Ann Jellicoe | Ann Jellicoe Keith Johnstone |
| 27 April | *Chips with Everything* | Arnold Wesker | John Dexter |
| 13 June | *Period of Adjustment* | Tennessee Williams | Roger Graef |
| 1 July | *The Captain's Hero** | Claus Hubalek Trans: Derek Goldby | Derek Goldby |
| 19 July | *Plays for England* | John Osborne | John Dexter Jonathan Miller |
| 11 Sept | *Brecht on Brecht* | George Tabori (Arr.) | John Bird |
| 16 Sept | *Day Of The Prince** | Frank Hilton | Keith Johnstone |
| 1 Nov | *Happy Days* | Samuel Beckett | George Devine |
| 3 Dec | *Mime* | Samy Molcho | Samy Molcho |
| 9 Dec | *The Pope's Wedding** | Edward Bond | Keith Johnstone |
| 18 Dec | *Squat Betty* and *The Sponge Room* | Keith Waterhouse and Willis Hall | John Dexter |

* 'Sunday Night' productions.

| Date | Play | Author | Director |
|------|------|--------|----------|
| **1963** | | | |
| 8 Jan | *Misalliance* | Bernard Shaw | Frank Hauser |
| 1 Feb | *Jackie the Jumper* | Gwyn Thomas | John Dexter |
| 6 Mar | *Diary of a Madman* | Gogol | Lindsay Anderson |
| 17 Mar | *Home To Now** | Negro Sketches, etc. Bari Jonson | Bari Jonson |
| 24 Mar | *In The Interests Of The State** | Vanessa Redgrave (Arr.) | |
| 4 April | *Naked* | Luigi Pirandello | David William |
| 7 April | *Skyvers** | Barry Reckord | Ann Jellicoe |
| 21 April | *Spring Awakening** | Frank Wedekind Trans: Tom Osborn | Desmond O'Donovan |
| 28 April | *First Results** | Mime, Clowning and Comic Improvisation | William Gaskill George Devine Claude Chagrin |
| 14 May | *Day of the Prince* | Frank Hilton | Keith Johnstone |
| 12 June | *Kelly's Eye* | Henry Livings | David Scase |
| 23 July | *Skyvers* | Barry Reckord | Ann Jellicoe |
| 28 July | *Wiley** | Mary McCormick | Elaine Pranksy |
| 12 Sept | *Exit the King* | Eugène Ionesco | George Devine |
| **1964** | | | |
| 12 Mar | *The Seagull* | Chekhov Trans: Ann Jellicoe | Tony Richardson |
| 15 Mar | *Edgware Road Blues** | Leonard Kingston | Keith Johnstone |
| 11 June | *St Joan of the Stockyards* | Bertolt Brecht Trans: Charlotte and A. L. Lloyd | Tony Richardson |
| 9 Sept | *Inadmissible Evidence* | John Osborne | Anthony Page |
| 22 Oct | *Cuckoo in the Nest* | Ben Travers | Anthony Page |
| 26 Nov | *Julius Caesar* | William Shakespeare | Lindsay Anderson |
| 30 Dec | *Waiting for Godot* | Samuel Beckett | Anthony Page |
| **1965** | | | |
| 28 Feb | *The Sleepers Den** | Peter Gill | Desmond O'Donovan |
| 11 Mar | *Happy End* | Kurt Weill and Bertolt Brecht | Michael Geliot |
| 19 April | *Spring Awakening* | Frank Wedekind Trans: Tom Osborn | Desmond O'Donovan |
| 2 May | *Miniatures** | David Cregan | Donald Howarth |
| 19 May | *Meals on Wheels* | Charles Wood | John Osborne |
| 30 June | *A Patriot for Me* | John Osborne | Anthony Page |
| 8 Aug | *A Collier's Friday Night** | D. H. Lawrence | Peter Gill |
| 28 Aug | *The World's Baby** | Michael Hastings | Patrick Dromgoole |
| 18 Oct | *Shelley* | Ann Jellicoe | Ann Jellicoe |
| 27 Oct | *The Cresta Run* | N. F. Simpson | Keith Johnstone |
| 3 Nov | *Saved* | Edward Bond | William Gaskill |
| 9 Dec | *Serjeant Musgrave's Dance* | John Arden | Jane Howell |
| 12 Dec | *Experiment** | Actors' Studio | Keith Johnstone |
| 20 Dec | *Clowning* | Keith Johnstone | Keith Johnstone |

* 'Sunday Night' productions.

| Date | Play | Author | Director |
|------|------|--------|----------|
| **1966** | | | |
| 13 Jan | *A Chaste Maid in Cheapside* | Thomas Middleton | William Gaskill |
| 16 Jan | *The Dancers* and *Transcending* | David Cregan | Jane Howell |
| 17 Feb | *The Knack* | Ann Jellicoe | Desmond O'Donovan |
| 3 Mar | *The Performing Giant* | Keith Johnstone | William Gaskill Keith Johnstone |
| 3 Mar | *Transcending* | David Cregan | Jane Howell |
| 27 Mar | *Little Guy, Napoleon* | Leonard Pluta | Tom Osborn |
| 27 Mar | *The Local Stigmatic* | Heathcote Williams | Peter Gill |
| 11 April | *The Voysey Inheritance* | Harley Granville-Barker | Jane Howell |
| 19 May | *Their Very Own and Golden City* | Arnold Wesker | William Gaskill |
| 5 June | *When Did You Last See My Mother* | Christopher Hampton | Robert Kidd |
| 26 June | *Bartleby* | Herman Melville | Massino Manuelli |
| 26 June | *The Local Stigmatic* | Heathcote Williams | Peter Gill |
| 21 July | *Ubu Roi* | Alfred Jarry Adapt: Iain Cuthbertson | Iain Cuthbertson |
| 21 Aug | *It's My Criminal* | Howard Brenton | Ian Watt Smith |
| 21 Aug | *The Ruffian on the Stair* | Joe Orton | Peter Gill |
| 30 Aug | *Bartholomew Fair* (presented by the National Youth Theatre) | Ben Jonson | Michael Croft |
| 12 Sept | *Little Malcolm and His Struggle Against the Eunuchs* (presented by the National Youth Theatre) | David Halliwell | Geoffrey Reeves |
| 21 Sept | *Three Men for Colverton* | David Cregan | Desmond O'Donovan |
| 20 Oct | *Macbeth* | William Shakespeare | William Gaskill |
| 30 Oct | *A Provincial Life* | Peter Gill | Peter Gill |
| 12 Dec | *The Lion and the Jewel* | Wole Soyinka | Desmond O'Donovan |
| **1967** | | | |
| 12 Jan | *The Soldier's Fortune* | Thomas Otway | Peter Gill |
| 23 Feb | *Roots* | Arnold Wesker | Jane Howell |
| 5 Mar | *A Touch of Brightness* | Partarp Sharma | Ian Watt Smith |
| 16 Mar | *The Daughter-in-Law* | D. H. Lawrence | Peter Gill |
| 19 Mar | *A View to the Common* | James Casey | Desmond O'Donovan |
| 18 April | *Three Sisters* | Chekhov Trans: Edward Bond | William Gaskill |
| 6 June | *Crimes of Passion (The Ruffian on the Stair; The Erpingham Camp)* | Joe Orton | Peter Gill |
| 20 June | *A View to the Common* | James Casey | Desmond O'Donovan |
| 4 July | *The Restoration of Arnold Middleton* | David Storey | Robert Kidd |
| 25 July | *OGODIVELEFTTHE-GASON* | Donald Howarth | Donald Howarth |

* 'Sunday Night' productions.

| Date | Play | Author | Director |
|------|------|--------|----------|
| **1967** | | | |
| 23 July | *Dance of the Teletape*• | Charles Hayward | Charles Hayward |
| 2 Aug | *America Hurrah* (The Open Theatre) | Jean-Claude van Itallie | Joseph Chaikin and Jacques Levy |
| 11 Sept | *Fill the Stage with Happy Hours* (E.S.C. production at the Vaudeville Theatre) | Charles Wood | William Gaskill |
| 8 Oct | *The Journey of the Fifth Horse*• | Ronald Ribman | Bill Bryden |
| 19 Oct | *Marya* | Isaac Babel Adapt: Christopher Hampton | Robert Kidd |
| 15 Nov | *Dingo* | Charles Wood | William Gaskill |
| 7 Dec | *The Dragon* | Yevgeny Schwarz Trans: Max Hayward and Harold Shukman | Jane Howell |
| 11 Dec | The Paperbag Players | | Judith Martin |
| **1968** | | | |
| 31 Jan | *Twelfth Night* | William Shakespeare | Jane Howell |
| 11 Feb | *Backbone*• | Michael Rosen | Bill Bryden |
| 29 Feb | *A Collier's Friday Night* | D. H. Lawrence | Peter Gill |
| 7 Mar | *The Daughter-in-Law* | D. H. Lawrence | Peter Gill |
| 14 Mar | *The Widowing of Mrs Holroyd* | D. H. Lawrence | Peter Gill |
| 31 Mar | *Early Morning*• | Edward Bond | William Gaskill |
| 28 April | *Funnyhouse of a Negro* and *A Lesson in Dead Language*• | Adrienne Kennedy | Rob Knights |
| 8 May | *Backbone* | Michael Rosen | Bill Bryden |
| 23 May | *Time Present* | John Osborne | Anthony Page |
| 3 July | *The Hotel in Amsterdam* | John Osborne | Anthony Page |
| 4 Aug | *Changing Lines*• | Nicholas Wright | Nicholas Wright |
| 21 Aug | *Trixie and Baba* | John Antrobus | Jane Howell |
| 11 Sept | *Total Eclipse* | Christopher Hampton | Robert Kidd |
| 2 Oct | *The Houses by the Green* | David Cregan | Jane Howell |
| 13 Oct | *The Tutor*• | Jakob Lenz and Bertolt Brecht Trans: Richard Grunberger | Barry Hanson |
| 29 Oct | *Look Back in Anger* | John Osborne | Anthony Page |
| 11 Dec | *This Story of Yours* | John Hopkins | Christopher Morahan |
| **1969** | | | |
| 9 Jan | *Life Price* | Jeremy Seabrook and Michael O'Neill | Peter Gill |
| 7 Feb | *Saved* | Edward Bond | William Gaskill |
| 19 Feb | *Narrow Road to the Deep North* | Edward Bond | Jane Howell |
| 13 Mar | *Early Morning* | Edward Bond | William Gaskill |
| 22 April | *In Celebration* | David Storey | Lindsay Anderson |

• 'Sunday Night' productions.

| Date | Play | Author | Director |
|------|------|--------|----------|
| **1969** | | | |
| 23 June | The Bread and Puppet Theatre | | Judith Martin |
| 6 July | *Captain Oates' Left Sock** | John Antrobus | Barry Hanson |
| 14 July | *The Double Dealer* | William Congreve | William Gaskill |
| 25 Sept | *L'Amante Anglaise* (Compagnie Renaud-Barrault) | Marguerite Duras | |
| 26 Sept | *Oh! Les Beaux Jours* (Compagnie Renaud-Barrault) | Samuel Beckett | |
| 20 Oct | *The Contractor* | David Storey | Lindsay Anderson |
| 9 Nov | *Famine** | Thomas Murphy | Clifford Williams |
| 26 Nov | *Insideout* | Frank Norman | Ken Campbell |
| 24 Dec | *The Three Musketeers Ride Again* | The Alberts Additional material: Donald Howarth | Eleanor Fazan |
| **1970** | | | |
| 28 Jan | *Three Months Gone* | Donald Howarth | Ronald Eyre |
| 1 Feb | *The Big Romance* | Robert Thornton | Roger Williams |
| 24 Feb | *Uncle Vanya* | Chekhov Version by Christopher Hampton from trans. by Nina Froud | Anthony Page |
| 14 April | *Widowers' Houses* | George Bernard Shaw | Michael Blakemore |
| 18 May | Cafe la Mama Theatre | | |
| 17 June | *Home* | David Storey | Lindsay Anderson |
| 3 Aug | *The Philanthropist* | Christopher Hampton | Robert Kidd |
| 14 Sept | *Cancer* | Michael Weller | Roger Hendricks Simon |
| 21 Oct | *Come Together Festival* | | |
| 11 Nov | *AC/DC* | Heathcote Williams | Nicholas Wright |
| **1971** | | | |
| 18 Jan | *The Duchess of Malfi* | John Webster | Peter Gill |
| 1 Mar | *Man is Man* | Bertolt Brecht | William Gaskill |
| 13 April | *One at Night* | Denis Cannan | Roger Williams |
| 24 May | *Slag* | David Hare | Max Stafford-Clark |
| 5 July | *The Lovers of Viorne* | Marguerite Duras | Jonathan Hales |
| 17 Aug | *West of Suez* | John Osborne | Anthony Page |
| 29 Sept | *Lear* | Edward Bond | William Gaskill |
| 9 Nov | *The Changing Room* | David Storey | Lindsay Anderson |
| **1972** | | | |
| 26 Jan | *Alpha Beta* | E. A. Whitehead | Anthony Page |
| 2 Mar | *Veterans* | Charles Wood | Ronald Eyre |
| 14 April | *Big Wolf* | Harald Mueller Trans: Steve Gooch | William Gaskill and Pam Brighton |
| 24 May | *Crete and Sergeant Pepper* | John Antrobus | Peter Gill |
| 28 June | *Hedda Gabler* | Henrik Ibsen Adapt. by John Osborne | Anthony Page |

* 'Sunday Night' productions.

| Date | Play | Author | Director |
|------|------|--------|----------|
| **1972** | | | |
| 8 Aug | *The Old Ones* | Arnold Wesker | John Dexter |
| 19 Sept | *Richard's Cork Leg* | Brendan Behan | Alan Simpson |
| 2 Nov | *A Pagan Place* | Edna O'Brien | Ronald Eyre |
| 6 Dec | *A Sense of Detachment* | John Osborne | Frank Dunlop |
| **1973** | | | |
| 16 Jan | *Krapp's Last Tape/Not I* | Samuel Beckett | Anthony Page |
| 27 Feb | *Freedom of the City* | Brian Friel | Albert Finney |
| 12 April | *Savages* | Christopher Hampton | Robert Kidd |
| 22 May | *The Sea* | Edward Bond | William Gaskill |
| 28 June | *Magnificence* | Howard Brenton | Max Stafford-Clark |
| 19 July | *The Removalists* | David Williamson | Jim Sharman |
| 15 Aug | *Cromwell* | David Storey | Anthony Page |
| 26 Sept | *The Farm* | David Storey | Lindsay Anderson |
| 7 Nov | *The Merry Go-Round* | D. H. Lawrence | Peter Gill |
| **1974** | | | |
| 2 Jan | *The Island* | Athol Fugard, John Kani and Winston Ntshona | Athol Fugard |
| 8 Jan | *Sizwe Bansi is Dead* | Athol Fugard, John Kani and Winston Ntshona | Athol Fugard |
| 22 Jan | *Statements After An Arrest Under The Immorality Act* | Athol Fugard | Athol Fugard |
| 11 Mar | *Runaway* | Peter Ransley | Alfred Lynch |
| 9 April | *Life Class* | David Storey | Lindsay Anderson |
| 5 June | *Tooth of Crime* | Sam Shepard | Jim Sharman |
| 16 July | *Play Mas* | Mustapha Matura | Donald Howarth |
| 14 Aug | *Bingo* | Edward Bond | Jane Howell |
| 9 Oct | *The Great Caper* | Ken Campbell | Nicholas Wright |
| 12 Nov | *The City* | The Tokyo Kid Brothers | Yutaka Higushi |
| **1975** | | | |
| 2 Jan | *Objections to Sex and Violence* | Cary Churchill | John Tydeman |
| 29 Jan | *Statements and Not I* | Athol Fugard Samuel Beckett | Anthony Page |
| 27 Feb | *Don's Party* | David Williamson | Michael Blakemore |
| 7 April | The Sunday Times Student Drama Festival | | |
| 17 April | *Entertaining Mr Sloane* | Joe Orton | Roger Croucher |
| 3 June | *Loot* | Joe Orton | Albert Finney |
| 16 July | *What The Butler Saw* | Joe Orton | Lindsay Anderson |

# Appendix B  Financial Tables

**Year ended 31 March, 1957**   Arts Council grant, including guarantees: £7,000

| PLAY | PERFS | SEATS % | BOX OFFICE % | PRODUCTION COSTS | BOX OFFICE TAKINGS |
|------|-------|---------|--------------|------------------|--------------------|
| *The Mulberry Bush* | 30 | 45 | 35·6 | | 2,757 |
| *The Crucible* | 32 | 45 | 39 | | 3,239 |
| *Don Juan and The Death of Satan* | 8 | 18 | 22 | 5,164* | 367 |
| *Look Back in Anger* | 151 | 67·8 | 59·8 | | 23,089 |
| *Cards of Identity* | 40 | 57·7 | 46 | | 4,836 |
| *Good Woman of Setzuan* | 46 | 55·3 | 59 | 2,421 | 6,687 |
| *The Country Wife* | 60 | 94·8 | 90 | 1,274 | 13,962 |
| *Member of the Wedding* | 37 | 41·4 | 39 | 1,728 | 3,743 |
| | 404 | 64·0 | 56 | 10,587 | 58,680 |

| | | |
|---|---|---|
| Overheads, Running costs | | 65,160 |
| Transfer, rights | | 8,505 |

112

* No individual figures kept.

**Year ended 31 March, 1958**  Arts Council grant, including guarantees: £5,000

| PLAY | PERFS | SEATS % | BOX OFFICE % | PRODUCTION COSTS | BOX OFFICE TAKINGS |
|---|---|---|---|---|---|
| *Fin de Partie and Acte Sans Parole* | 6 | 65 | 69 | 723 | |
| *The Entertainer* | 36 | 98 | 100 | 1,509 | |
| *The Apollo de Bellac and The Chairs* | 30 | 42 | 33 | 1,418 | |
| *The Making of Moo* | 30 | 49 | 40 | 1,755 | |
| *Look Back in Anger* (first revival) | 104 | 78 | 68 | | |
| *The Chairs* (revival) and | | | | | |
| *How Can We Save Father?* | 8 | 40 | 31 | 857 | |
| *Nekrassov* | 46 | 58 | 50 | 2,260 | |
| *Requiem for a Nun* | 30 | 89 | 86 | 1,311 | |
| *Lysistrata* | 53 | 98 | 90 | 2,925 | |
| *Epitaph for George Dillon* | 38 | 52 | 46 | 1,144 | |
| *The Sport of my Mad Mother* | 14 | 35 | 23 | 872 | |
| | 395 | 70 | 63·8 | 14,774 | 65,289 |
| Overheads, Running costs | | | | 77,293 | |
| Transfer, rights | | | | | 39,631 |

113

**Year ended 31 March, 1959** Arts Council grant, including guarantees: £5,500

| PLAY | | PERFS | SEATS % | BOX OFFICE % | PRODUCTION COSTS | BOX OFFICE TAKINGS |
|---|---|---|---|---|---|---|
| A Resounding Tinkle and The Hole | | 28 | 51 | 41 | 679 | 3,105 |
| Epitaph for George Dillon | | 24 | 53 | 41 | N.A. | 2,710 |
| Flesh to a Tiger | | 29 | 22 | 15 | 2,783 | 1,196 |
| The Chairs and The Lesson | | 45 | 72 | 53 | 548 | 7,408 |
| Gay Landscape | Guest | 8 | 17 | 12 | N.A. | 268 |
| Chicken Soup with Barley | Rep | 8 | 40 | 26 | N.A. | 565 |
| The Private Prosecutor | Season | 8 | 18 | 31 | N.A. | 290 |
| Dear Augustine | | 8 | 26 | 19 | N.A. | 410 |
| Major Barbara | | 36 | 58 | 49 | 1,699 | 4,810 |
| Live Like Pigs | | 22 | 34 | 25 | 1,778 | 1,486 |
| End Game and Krapp's Last Tape | | 38 | 40 | 28 | 529 | 2,853 |
| Moon on a Rainbow Shawl† | | 35 | 48 | 37 | | 3,538 |
| The Long and the Short and the Tall‡ | | 94 | 70 | 59 | 2,270 | 14,952 |
| | | 383 | 53 | 42 | 10,308 | 52,141* |
| Overheads, Running costs | | | | | 78,447 | |
| Transfer, rights | | | | | | 18,507 |

† Moon on a Rainbow Shawl was a Tennents Ltd. Production.
‡ The Long and the Short and the Tall concluded its run at the Royal Court Theatre with 100 performances on 4 April, 1959 and transferred to the New Theatre the next week.
N.A. Not Available.
* Adjusted after audit.

114

## Year ended 31 March, 1960    Arts Council grant, including guarantees: £5,000

| PLAY | PERFS | SEATS % | BOX OFFICE % | PRODUCTION COSTS | BOX OFFICE TAKINGS |
|---|---|---|---|---|---|
| *Sugar in the Morning* | 28 | 36 | 28 | 1,153 | 2,104 |
| *Orpheus Descending* | 52 | 64 | 53 | 2,728 | 7,461 |
| *Roots* | 31 | 74 | 66 | 831 | 5,543 |
| *Look After Lulu* | 45 | 97·5 | 93·6 | 4,381 | 12,603 |
| *Cock-a-Doodle-Dandy* | 36 | 60 | 49 | 2,316 | 4,747 |
| *Serjeant Musgrave's Dance* | 28 | 30 | 21 | 2,088 | 1,578 |
| *Rosmersholm* | 37 | 100 | 93 | 2,150 | 9,343 |
| *One Way Pendulum* | 37 | 93 | 87 | 2,042 | 8,700 |
| *The Lily White Boys* | 45 | 68 | 59 | 2,620 | 7,222 |
| *The Room* and *The Dumb Waiter* | 22 | 40 | 30 | 785 | 1,818 |
| *The Naming of Murderers' Rock*† | 2 | 22 | 19 | 1,952 | 106 |
| | 369 | 69 | 61 | 23,046 | 63,233* |
| Overheads, Running costs | | | | 83,261 | |
| Transfer, rights | | | | | 19,653 |

† *The Naming of Murderers' Rock* continued to run until 16 April, 1960:

    Total of run for 20 performances    506
    Average per performance    25
    Percentage of capacity    9%

* Total adjusted after audit.

## Year ended 31 March, 1961  Arts Council grant, including guarantees: £8,000

| PLAY | PERFS | SEATS % | BOX OFFICE % | PRODUCTION COSTS | BOX OFFICE TAKINGS |
|---|---|---|---|---|---|
| *The Naming of Murderers' Rock* | 18 | 12 | 8 | | 399 |
| *Rhinoceros* | 44 | 100 | 99 | 4,953 | 16,372 |
| *Chicken Soup with Barley* | 22 | 90 | 82·5 | 1,509 | 4,917 |
| *Roots* | 30 | 100 | 93 | 1,120 | 7,553 |
| *I'm Talking About Jerusalem* | 29 | 71·4 | 63 | 1,138 | 4,966 |
| *The Wesker Trilogy* | 24 | 83·6 | 75 | | 4,870 |
| (the three plays in repertory) | | | | | |
| *The Happy Haven* | 21 | 18 | 12 | 1,720 | 706 |
| *Platonov* | 44 | 91 | 84·5 | 3,624 | 13,986 |
| *Trials by Logue* | 21 | 30 | 22 | 2,206 | 1,260 |
| *The Lion in Love* | 28 | 49 | 40 | 1,318 | 3,049 |
| *The Importance of Being Oscar*† | 32 | 98·7 | 90 | N.A. | 10,877 |
| *The Changeling* | 30 | 60 | 47·7 | N.A. | 5,386 |
| *Jacques*‡ | 10 | 28 | 19·7 | | 614 |
| | 353 | 72·4 | 67·4 | 17,588 | 74,955 |
| Overheads, Running costs | | | | 86,449 | |
| Transfer, rights | | | | | 7,888 |

† *The Importance of Being Oscar* is a visiting company and not an English Stage Company production.

‡ *Jacques* completed its run in 1962.

**Year ended 31 March, 1962**  Arts Council grant, including guarantees: £8,000

| PLAY | PERFS | SEATS % | BOX OFFICE % | PRODUCTION COSTS | BOX OFFICE TAKINGS |
|---|---|---|---|---|---|
| *Altona* | 45 | 89 | 80 | 4,024 | 11,225 |
| *Jacques*† | 18 | 24·6 | 15 | | 847 |
| *The Blacks* | 30 | 41 | 30 | 3,690 | 2,806 |
| *The Kitchen* | 86 | 70·6 | 60·7 | 2,051 | 16,226 |
| *Luther* | 28 | 100 | 96 | 6,421 | 10,089 |
| *August for the People* | 15 | 89 | 82 | 4,227 | 4,632 |
| *The American Dream* and | | | | | |
| *The Death of Bessie Smith* | 22 | 46·4 | 35·4 | 2,256 | 2,423 |
| *That's Us*‡ | 7 | 13·7 | 9·9 | | 216 |
| *The Keep* (first run) | 29 | 80·5 | 72 | 2,093 | 6,496 |
| *The Fire Raisers* and *Box and Cox* | 36 | 57·2 | 46·6 | 3,288 | 5,216 |
| *Midsummer Night's Dream* | 29 | 40·5 | 22·7 | 4,201 | 2,408 |
| *The Keep* (second run) | 38 | 77·6 | 70 | | 8,263 |
| *The Knack*§ | 6 | 56·5 | 45 | 1,518 | 841 |
| | 389 | 67·0 | 57·0 | 33,769 | 72,960 |

*Less:* production costs shared by
  associated companies:

Altona · · · · · · · · · · 2,012
Luther · · · · · · · · · · 3,210
August for the People · · · · · · · · · 1,409

     6,631
     27,138

Overheads, Running costs
    Transfer, rights     97,989

           26,724

† *Jacques* production costs under 1961 budget.

‡ Cambridge Arts Theatre production.

§ *The Knack* continued its run in 1962–3.

117

## Year ended 31 March, 1963  Arts Council grant, including guarantees: £20,000

| PLAY | PERFS | SEATS % | BOX OFFICE % | PRODUCTION COSTS | BOX OFFICE TAKINGS |
|---|---|---|---|---|---|
| *The Knack*† | 23 | 64 | 49 | 4,158 | 3,526 |
| *Chips with Everything* | 51 | 94 | 85 | 2,937 | 13,452 |
| *Period of Adjustment* | 29 | 74 | 66 | 6,007 | 5,962 |
| *Plays for England* | 60 | 71 | 58 | 2,189 | 13,193 |
| *Brecht on Brecht* | 54 | 73 | 64 | 1,769 | 10,734 |
| *Happy Days* | 35 | 49 | 36 | | 3,905 |
| *Mime* | 12 | 27 | 19 | | 711 |
| *The Sponge Room and Squat Betty* | 20 | 16·6 | 12 | 2,627 | 752 |
| *Misalliance* | 21 | 47 | 36 | N.A. | 2,364 |
| *Jackie the Jumper* | 27 | 28 | 17 | 4,921 | 1,704 |
| *Diary of a Madman* | 28 | 35 | 24 | 2,935 | 2,067 |
| | 360 | 60 | 49·6 | | 58,370 |
| *Naked* | | | | 3,136 | |
| Overheads, Running costs | | | | 30,669 | |
| | | | | 80,433 | |
| Transfer, rights | | | | | 20,038 |

† *The Knack* production costs under 1962 budget.

118

## Year ended 31 March, 1964      Arts Council grant, including guarantees: £20,000

| PLAY | PERFS | SEATS % | BOX OFFICE % | PRODUCTION COSTS | BOX OFFICE TAKINGS |
|---|---|---|---|---|---|
| *Day of the Prince* | 28 | 25 | 18·1 | 2,370 | 1,748 |
| *Naked* | 37 | 38 | 28·7 | | 3,665 |
| *Kelly's Eye* | 20 | 24 | 17·0 | 3,096 | 1,178 |
| *Skyvers* | 22 | 33·5 | 22·5 | 1,422 | 1,710 |
| *Exit the King* | 60 | 100 | 93·2 | 2,908 | 12,295 |
| *The Milk Train Doesn't Stop Here Anymore*† | | | | 2,072 | |
| *Chips with Everything*‡ | 28 | 76·4 | 66·8 | | 6,462 |
| | 195 | 59·3 | 50·6 | 11,869 | 34,996 |
| Overheads, Running costs | | | | 69,269 | |
| Transfer, rights | | | | | 16,801 |

† Production abandoned.

‡ Pre-U.S.A. production. The entire cost was borne by the U.S.A. presenter.

**Year ended 27 March, 1965†   Arts Council grant, including guarantees: £32,500**

| PLAY | PERFS | SEATS % | BOX OFFICE % | PRODUCTION COSTS | BOX OFFICE TAKINGS |
|---|---|---|---|---|---|
| *Inadmissible Evidence* ‡ | 40 | 98 | 95·4 | 3,003 | 11,890 |
| *A Cuckoo in the Nest*† | 36 | 45 | 42 | 3,629 | 4,727 |
| *Julius Caesar* | 28 | 71 | 53·4 | 5,055 | 4,387 |
| *Waiting for Godot* | 69 | 81 | 73 | 2,164 | 14,856 |
| *Happy End*§ | 20 | 68·6 | 65 | 4,874 | 4,608 |
| | 193 | 74·7 | 68·4 | 18,727 | 40,468 |
| Overheads, Running costs | | | | 65,637 | |
| Transfer, rights | | | | | 12,076 |

† The Royal Court was closed for redecoration until 9 September, 1964.

‡ *Inadmissible Evidence* in association with John Osborne Productions, Ltd.

§ *Happy End* continued its run in 1965–6. In association with Bridge Productions, Ltd.

## 28 March, 1965 to 2 October, 1965   Arts Council grant, including guarantees: £50,555

| PLAY | PERFS | SEATS % | BOX OFFICE % | PRODUCTION COSTS | BOX OFFICE TAKINGS |
|---|---|---|---|---|---|
| *Happy End* | 16 | 61 | 52 | | 2,952 |
| *Spring Awakening* | 32 | 60 | 52 | 4,279 | 4,892 |
| *Meals on Wheels* | 19 | 17 | 17 | 3,485 | 1,021 |
| *A Patriot for Me* | 53 | 92·5 | 94·4 | 12,506 | 17,516 |
| | 120 | 69 | 66·8 | 20,270 | 26,381 |

### 4 October, 1965 to 2 April, 1966 Gaskill Season

| PLAY | PERFS | SEATS % | BOX OFFICE % | PRODUCTION COSTS | BOX OFFICE TAKINGS |
|---|---|---|---|---|---|
| *Shelley* | 19 | 44 | 28·1 | 1,799 | 1,799 |
| *Cresta Run* | 19 | 41 | 26·5 | 2,118 | 1,689 |
| *Saved* | 24 | 50 | 36·7 | 1,180 | 3,051 |
| *Serjeant Musgrave's Dance* | 32 | 61 | 49·0 | 1,602 | 5,259 |
| *Clowning* | 15 | 22 | 9·7 | 454 | 507 |
| *A Chaste Maid in Cheapside* | 25 | 52 | 39·7 | 2,122 | 3,325 |
| *The Knack* | 19 | 43 | 29·8 | 1,230 | 1,907 |
| *Performing Giant* and *Transcending* | 19 | 22 | 11·3 | 1,328 | 421 |
| | 164 | 42 | 32 | 11,813 | 17,958 |
| Dress rehearsals | 15 | | | | 1,608 |
| | 179 | | | | 28,916 |

Overheads, Running costs  117,896

Transfer, rights  26,537

**Year ended 1 April, 1967**   Arts Council grant, including guarantees: £88,650

| PLAY | PERFS | SEATS % | BOX OFFICE % | PRODUCTION COSTS | BOX OFFICE TAKINGS |
|---|---|---|---|---|---|
| *Serjeant Musgrave's Dance*† | 13 | 45.4 | 34.8 | | 1,512 |
| *The Voysey Inheritance* | 55 | 46.4 | 41.2 | 3,024 | 7,588 |
| *Their Very Own and Golden City* | 26 | 52.8 | 40.1 | 2,861 | 3,590 |
| *Ubu Roi* | 39 | 45.4 | 38.3 | 4,565 | 4,616 |
| *Three Men for Colverton* | 26 | 35.7 | 27.1 | 3,721 | 2,372 |
| *Macbeth* (Guinness & Signoret)‡ | 32 | 97.7 | 98.1 | 6,181 | 12,098 |
| *Macbeth* (Roeves & Engel) | 16 | 71.0 | 42.9 | | 2,308 |
| *The Lion and the Jewel* | 27 | 57.5 | 48.9 | 4,624 | 4,398 |
| *The Soldier's Fortune* | 39 | 62.4 | 52.3 | 5,160 | 6,846 |
| *Roots* | 18 | 86.0 | 63.5 | 2,967 | 3,828 |
| *Roots* (school matinées)‡ | 6 | 88.0 | 82.7 | | 646 |
| *The Daughter-in-Law*§ | 17 | 58.5 | 46.0 | 2,426 | 2,622 |
| | 306 | | 50.0 | 35,529 | 52,424 |
| Overheads, Running costs | | | | 110,198 | |
| Transfer, rights | | | | | 714 |

† *Serjeant Musgrave's Dance* opened in the Financial Year 1965–6, and took in a total of 7,724 for 45 performances (45%) and seating 59.5%.

‡ School Matinées are at reduced prices, hence reduced financial capacity.

§ *The Daughter-in-Law* continued its run to April 8, 1967, and took in a total of 4,010 (48%), seating 61.1%.

## Year ended 30 March, 1968    Arts Council grant, including guarantees: £100,000

| PLAY | PERFS | SEATS % | BOX OFFICE % | PRODUCTION COSTS | BOX OFFICE TAKINGS |
|---|---|---|---|---|---|
| The Daughter-in-Law | 8 | 67·7 | 51·5 | 5,061 | 1,388 |
| Three Sisters | 53 | 90·6 | 75·2 |  | 13,542 |
| Crimes of Passion | 15 | 41·3 | 28·3 | 1,683 | 1,428 |
| A View to the Common | 15 | 22·8 | 14·3 | 1,084 | 707 |
| The Restoration of Arnold Middleton | 22 | 71·2 | 59·6 | 1,287 | 4,373 |
| OGODIVELEFTTHEGASON | 8 | 46·6 | 33·2 | 2,120 | 889 |
| Fill the Stage with Happy Hours† | 32 | 36·1 | 44·9 | 3,543 | 4,817 |
| Marya | 25 | 64·1 | 54·3 | 3,429 | 4,615 |
| Dingo | 19 | 32·5 | 25·6 | 2,541 | 1,634 |
| The Dragon | 38 | 38·5 | 31·5 | 6,099 | 3,977 |
| Twelfth Night | 26 | 90·9 | 66·8 | 5,515 | 5,819 |
| (school matinées) | 5 |  |  |  | 577 |
| A Collier's Friday Night‡ | 9 | 72·5 | 57·0 | 8,408 | 1,740 |
| The Daughter-in-Law‡ | 8 | 79·8 | 63·0 |  | 1,689 |
| The Widowing of Mrs Holroyd‡ | 10 | 87·7 | 74·3 |  | 2,481 |
|  | 293 | 61·6 | 50·1 | 39,220 | 50,178 |
| _Add:_ Dress rehearsal | | | | | 1,811 |
| Abortive production costs | | | | 680 | 51,989 |
|  | | | | 39,900 | |
| Overheads, Running costs | | | | 108,849 | |
| Transfer, rights | | | | | 2,115 |

† Played at the Vaudeville.

‡ Lawrence Repertory which continued its run to 4 May, 1968, had the following figures to 30 March: Takings: 65·3%; Seats Sold: 80·1%.

**1968–9** Arts Council grant, including guarantees: £94,000

| PLAY | PERFS | SEATS % | BOX OFFICE % | PRODUCTION COSTS | BOX OFFICE TAKINGS |
|---|---|---|---|---|---|
| D. H. Lawrence Season (from 1967–8) | 34 | 88·9 | 76·3 | † | 8,683 |
| Backbone | 12 | 51·6 | 41·6 | 2,182 | 1,685 |
| Time Present | 39 | 82·5 | 75·5 | 4,708 | 11,371 |
| The Hotel in Amsterdam | 47 | 98·4 | 96·2 | 5,204 | 17,495 |
| Trixie and Baba | 19 | 30·2 | 22·5 | 2,059 | 1,608 |
| Total Eclipse | 19 | 59·9 | 45·0 | 2,270 | 3,241 |
| Houses by the Green | 19 | 26·0 | 18·6 | 2,666 | 1,343 |
| Look Back in Anger | 52 | 89·5 | 66·9 | 3,944 | 13,114 |
| This Story of Yours | 24 | 51·8 | 43·1 | 3,500 | 3,909 |
| Life Price | 11 | 22·0 | 14·4 | 5,588 | 596 |
| Life Price—free seats | 14 | | | | 135 |
| Saved | 18 | 62·5 | 43·0 | 5,248 | 2,929 |
| Narrow Road to the Deep North | 19 | 44·2 | 28·6 | 7,493 | 2,032 |
| Early Morning | 13 | 52·0 | 35·6 | 5,832 | 1,746 |
| | 340 | 69·1 | 57·2 | 50,694 | 69,887 |
| Overheads, Running costs | | | | 123,801 | |
| Transfer, rights | | | | | 13,615 |

† Carried on 1967–8 budget.

**Year ended 4 April, 1970   Arts Council grant, including guarantees: £94,000**

| PLAY | PERFS | SEATS % | BOX OFFICE % | PRODUCTION COSTS | BOX OFFICE TAKINGS |
|---|---|---|---|---|---|
| *Saved* | 13 | 41·7 | 25·2 | | 1,248 |
| *In Celebration* | 67 | 75·0 | 62·0 | 3,423 | 15,692 |
| *Double Dealer* | 37 | 48·2 | 37·0 | 6,969 | 5,190 |
| *Bread and Puppet Theatre* | 17 | 53·2 | 30·0 | 385 | 1,925 |
| *Saved* | 7 | 53·5 | 35·1 | | 931 |
| *Narrow Road* } Prior to European Tour | 7 | 38·2 | 26·0 | | 668 |
| *Madeleine Renaud Season* | 11 | 83·0 | 65·3 | | 2,726 |
| *The Contractor* | 33 | 72·7 | 57·6 | 4,788 | 7,192 |
| *Insideout* | 26 | 40·7 | 28·0 | 4,681 | 2,773 |
| *Three Musketeers* | 28 | 30·7 | 23·7 | 4,751 | 2,507 |
| *Three Months Gone* | 25 | 79·5 | 69·9 | 4,235 | 6,590 |
| *Uncle Vanya* | 45 | 98·1 | 96·5 | 7,398 | 21,440 |
| | 316 | 64·9 | 57·6 | 36,630 | 68,882 |
| Overheads, Running costs | | | | 141,656 | |
| Transfer, rights | | | | | 2,609 |

# Year ended 3 April, 1971 Arts Council grant, excluding guarantees: £89,000*

| PLAY | PERFS | SEATS % | BOX OFFICE % | PRODUCTION COSTS | BOX OFFICE TAKINGS |
|------|-------|---------|--------------|------------------|--------------------|
| *Widowers' Houses* | 39 | 61·3 | 50·5 | 2,387 | 7,593 |
| *Cafe La Mama* | 19 | 51·0 | 33·9 | 812 | 2,465 |
| *Home* | 40 | 92·7 | 94·0 | 3,923 | 16,559 |
| *The Philanthropist* | 39 | 88·8 | 82·0 | 4,139 | 14,036 |
| *Cancer* | 36 | 42·2 | 29·7 | 4,425 | 4,722 |
| *Come Together Festival* | 19 | 76·0 | 31·0 | 5,357 | 2,446 |
| *AC/DC* | 16 | 32·0 | 20·0 | 1,326 | 1,378 |
| *Lulu* | 35 | 86·0 | 79·0 | 4,751 | 12,217 |
| *The Duchess of Malfi* | 38 | 60·7 | 39·5 | 5,749 | 6,618 |
| *Man is Man* | 38 | 55·0 | 40·0 | 4,807 | 6,752 |
| | 319 | 67·7 | 54·3 | 37,676 | 86,536 |
| Overheads, Running costs | | | | 144,806 | |
| Transfers, rights | | | | | 40,372 |

*Note: There was a £7,000 guarantee against loss which was not claimable as a surplus was made.

126

**Year ended 3 April, 1972**   Arts Council grant, excluding guarantees: £91,250*

| PLAY | PERFS | SEATS % | BOX OFFICE % | PRODUCTION COSTS | BOX OFFICE TAKINGS |
|---|---|---|---|---|---|
| *One At Night* | 33 | 39·0 | 28·2 | 4,779 | 4,090 |
| *Slag* | 39 | 92·0 | 82·0 | 5,240 | 14,087 |
| *The Lovers of Viorne* | 38 | 50·2 | 41·0 | 2,627 | 6,862 |
| *West of Suez* | 32 | 97·0 | 92·0 | 8,365 | 13,870 |
| *Lear* | 37 | 60·0 | 45·0 | 10,819 | 7,873 |
| *The Changing Room* | 39 | 94·0 | 89·0 | 7,943 | 16,041 |
| *Alpha Beta* | 39 | 96·7 | 88·0 | 5,963 | 16,368 |
| *Veterans* | 31 | 94·5 | 86·0 | 7,798 | 12,564 |
| | 288 | 78·2 | 68·8 | 53,534 | 91,755 |
| Overheads, Running costs | | | | 158,544 | |
| Transfers, rights | | | | | 39,599 |

*Note: There was a £8,750 guarantee against loss which was not claimable as a surplus was made.

# Sources Consulted

## Books

Brown, Ivor, *Theatre, 1954–5*, Max Reinhardt, 1955.
Brown, Ivor, *Theatre, 1955–6*, Max Reinhardt, 1956.
Dennis, Nigel; Spark, Muriel; Wilson, Angus; introduction by Eric Rhode. *Novelist's Theatre*, Penguin Books, 1966.
Duncan, Ronald, *How To Make Enemies*, Rupert Hart-Davis, 1968.
Esslin, Martin, *Reflections: Essays on Modern Theatre*, Doubleday and Company, Inc., New York, 1969.
Guildersleeve, Virginia C. *Government Regulation of the Elizabethan Drama*, The Columbia University Press, New York, 1908.
Hartnoll, Phyllis, ed. *The Oxford Companion to the Theatre*, Oxford University Press, 1967.
Herbert, A. P., *No Fine on Fun*, Methuen and Company, Ltd, 1957.
Landstone, Charles, *Off-Stage*, Elek Books, Ltd, 1953.
MacCarthy, Desmond, *The Court Theatre, 1904–1907*, A. H. Bullen, 1964.
Mander, Raymond, and Mitchenson, Joe, *The Theatres of London*, Rupert Hart-Davis, 1963.
Saint-Denis, Michel; introduction by Sir Laurence Olivier. *Theatre: The Rediscovery of Style*, Heinemann Educational Books, Ltd, 1960.
Sherriffs, Ronald Everett, (a Historical Study of the Development of Governmental Support to Theatre in Great Britain'. Unpublished Ph.D. dissertation. University of Southern California, 1963.
Taylor, John Russell, *Anger and After*, Penguin Books, 1962.
Tschudin, Marcus, *A Writer's Theatre: George Devine and the English Stage Company at the Royal Court 1956–1965*. Berne, Switzerland: European University Papers, 1973.
*Who's Who*, A. and C. Black, 1968.
*Who's Who in the Theatre*, Pitman Publishing, 1972.

## Periodicals

*Chelsea News, West London Press and Westminster and Pimlico News.*
*Daily Express* (London).
*Daily Mail* (London).
*Daily Mirror* (London).
*Daily Sketch* (London).
*Daily Telegraph* (London).

*Evening Standard* (London).
*Financial Times* (London).
*Glasgow Herald* (Glasgow, Scotland).
*Guardian* (London).
*Listener* (London).
*Liverpool Daily Post* (Liverpool, England).
*Manchester Guardian* (Manchester, England).
*New Society*.
*New Statesman*.
*News Chronicle* (London).
*Observer*.
*Plays and Players*.
*Sheffield Telegraph* (Sheffield, England).
*The Stage*.
*Star* (London).
*Sun* (London).
*Sunday Telegraph* (London).
*Sunday Times* (London).
*Tablet* (London).
*The Times* (London).
*Tribune* (London).
*Universe*.

## Interviews

Anderson, Lindsay
Andrews, Dennis
Blacksell, J. Edward, M.B.E.
Blatchley, John
Blond, Neville, C.M.G., O.B.E.
Brenton, Howard
Brighton, Pamela
Capon, Suzanna
Catty, Jon
Croucher, Roger
Davy, Antonia
Duncan, Ronald
Esslin, Martin
Fox, Robin, M.C.
Gaskill, William
Hampton, Christopher
Herbert, Jocelyn
Lawrence, Patricia
Lewenstein, Oscar
Osborne, John
Poke, Greville
Richardson, Tony
Rosen, Michael
Shaw, Glen Byam
Stafford-Clark, Max
Wright, Nicholas
Young, B. A.

## Other Sources

*The Arts Council of Great Britain, Annual Reports, 1945/46–1972/73,* The Arts Council of Great Britain, 1946–1973.

*The Arts Council of Great Britain: What It Is and What It Does,* The Arts Council of Great Britain, 1969.

*The Theatre Today in England and Wales,* The Arts Council of Great Britain, 1970.

*The Charter of Incorporation Granted by Her Majesty the Queen to the Arts Council of Great Britain, Seventh Day of February, 1967,* Her Majesty's Stationary Office, 1967.

Devine, George, 'Resignation Speech.' English Stage Company archives, n.d.

English Stage Company initial brochure. From the author's collection. Proof-reader's date: 5 April 1955.

English Stage Company memorandum on artistic policy. Dated 20 May 1960.

English Stage Company minutes of the joint meeting of the Artistic and Management Committees, 2 June 1966.

English Stage Company minutes of the meetings of the Council, January 1956–April 1970.

English Stage Company minutes of the meetings of the Management Committee, January 1956–April 1970.

English Stage Company notes on the Cambridge Arts Scheme. Dated 6 January 1961.

English Stage Company Policy Statement for the year 1966–7. Dated 31 March 1966.

Evidence submitted by the English Stage Company to the Estimates Committee (Sub-Committee B), House of Commons, 1969.

*Joint Committee on Censorship of the Theatre; Report.* Her Majesty's Stationary Office, 1967.

*The Provision of Theatre for Young People in Great Britain.* The Arts Council of Great Britain, 1966.

*Ten Years at the Royal Court, 1956–1966.* The English Stage Company, 1966.

# Index

134 *Index*